A Male/Female Continuum

Paths to Colleagueship

Carol Pierce
David Wagner
Bill Page

Library of Congress Catalogue Card Number 88-092431
ISBN 0-929767-02-0 pbk
© Copyright 1986, 1988
Second edition, expanded, 1994, 1998, 2004
All rights reserved.
Printed in The United States of America

NEW DYNAMICS Publications
P.O. Box 595
Laconia, New Hampshire 03247-0595

To all who are on their
gender journeys.

C ONTENTS

Preface   vii

Chapter 1   Introduction to the Journeys   1

Chapter 2   Men and Dominance   7

Chapter 3   Women and Subordinance   13

Chapter 4   Women in Transition   19

Chapter 5   Men in Transition   27

Chapter 6   Reflections on the Continuum So Far   37

Chapter 7   Colleagueship   47

Chapter 8   Looking Ahead on our Journeys   59

Notes   65

Suggested Reading   67

The Male/Female Continuum graphic

PREFACE TO THE EXPANDED EDITION

We are delighted with the continued demand for this book. We are encouraged and troubled by the continuing need for its guidance in a new century since the concepts of the book first emerged in our work starting in the 1970's. We have long talked about the multigenerational change that this book addresses, yet a hope for pervasive and durable gender equity in our lifetime has underpinned our work. The voices of the 19th century feminists echoed and given new voice by women and men throughout the world today, tell us that we are part of the persistent march for human equality that stretches beyond present generations. Yet, we know that the future is created in the present and invite you to join us in the continuing unfolding of gender equity in the context of justice and individual freedom. We advocate this knowing, in the words of Amartya Sen, "Indeed, whether or not freedom enters *individual* well-being, individual freedom can be seen as being constituative of the goodness of *the society* which we have reasons to pursue[1]."

We note major ups and downs in the changes in our society since we and our New Dynamics colleagues consciously began the thought that developed into this continuum. The accomplishments in politics, law, domestic violence, employment, the arts, women's health, and the evolution of the sense of the spiritual in the years since the writing began on the first edition of this book are remarkable.

---

[1] Amartya Sen, *Inequality Reexamined*, (Cambridge, MA: Harvard University Press, paperback edition, 2002), 151.

We can say in reflection that what we are living through is what it is like to move a whole society away from dominance and subordinance to addressing male/female, multicultural, sexual orientation, class, age, and differently abled issues all at the same time. There is no going back. Too much has changed. We are excited by the expanding number of men and women working to continue the change process.

We are pleased that so many have found the Male/Female Continuum a useful tool for bringing clarity to the personal, organizational, and cultural processes of change we are experiencing. The response has been affirming. To bring perspective and compassion to our journeys as women and men is important. Our goal is to facilitate and keep open the dialogue between men and women, as we each focus on who we are and the context in which we live. Peace and justice are central to our work.

Through our work and our own experience we now know more about the journeys of women and men to colleagueship. This expanded edition of *The Male/Female Continuum: Paths to Colleagueship* reflects our growing understanding and perspectives. We note especially some of the diversity of experience of people of color and gay, lesbian, and bisexual people.

This book describes the stages of our gender journeys in a concise overview. We may not give as many examples in the text as readers might wish. A strength—and at the same time a weakness—of this book is its brevity. Other writers go into more depth on the various parts of this continuum. Some readers have told us that the book does not always read quickly because there is so much to think about. Each reader will have their own life experience to integrate into what is given here. We hope you will reflect on what we have written and use what is useful to you on your journey.

We have chosen to change little in this new printing, leaving to you the reader to supply the present and future context that fits your journey. This current printing finds only the updating of this Preface, Acknowledgements, dates, and New Dynamics Publications.

ACKNOWLEDGMENTS

We three authors are heterosexual and white. Insights and connections to diversity issues beyond gender were made possible for us through our work with people of color, lesbians, gay men, bisexual people, people of other diversities, and other white people in our client systems and colleague networks. We thank you all. We give special appreciation to our New Dynamics associates for the intensity of learning about our whiteness and straightness which was possible only because they are so fully who they are. We particularly thank our colleagues of color for conversations that helped to expand our comments on the journeys of people of color; and our lesbian, gay, and bisexual colleagues for conversations concerning the interaction of gender and sexual orientation issues.

Present and past New Dynamics partners directly involved in the early development of this continuum are Harriet Forkey, Richard Orange, Karen Terninko, Bill Gregory, and the authors. We wish to thank the partners, associates, and colleagues who have read this version and responded with their input or with whom we have talked. They are Linda Thomas, Heather Wishik, Barbara Berry, Lennox Joseph, Kiyoko Kasai Fujiu, Sharon Bueno Washington, Warren Oster, Jules Auger, and Helen Turnbull.

We each express appreciation to our family and friends for their support. We thank Kathryn Gohl for her editorial skills. Special thanks to Melanie Heinis for the contribution of her computer skills.

Carol Pierce
David Wagner
Bill Page

Introduction to the Journeys

The Maenka West African tribe has a saying, "If you force people to be the same, the only way left for them to be different is to try to get on top of one another."[1] We are on journeys to value our differences and to dismantle the way we have lived with dominance and subordinance.

Historically, we live in a system of dominance and subordinance whereby some people are given more power by birthright than others. Those who manage to escape this dynamic live outside the mainstream of culture handed down through generations. Still, we are moving away from unquestioning acceptance of power differentials. Over the last two hundred years in particular, group after group and nation after nation have sought and continue to seek equity in relation to others. The major change has been in how power is viewed and managed.

Currently, we are in a process where many men and women are seeking new ways to behave. Power relationships between us are drastically changing. The authors have created a diagram of this process—a Male/Female Continuum that shows

women's and men's journeys away from the dominance and subordinance of role stereotyping, into

the transition, during which women and men learn new ways to relate, and into

discovering colleagueship, where mutuality and empowerment of everyone make each one powerful and whole.

The Male/Female Continuum is displayed as a pull-out chart at the end of the book. The top line shows the movement of men on a journey

1) from the need to control women through the use of violence and sexual exploitation, to sexual harassment, to discrimination and courtesy (the orange section),

2) into a transition where at first they experience anger for having to change, then accept that there is much to learn about expanding the dimensions of being male (the blue section),

3) and on into colleagueship where how tasks are accomplished is as important as the task itself (the green section).

The bottom line shows the journey for women. They move, as subordinants,*

1) from the use of violent retaliation, focused at both themselves and men, and psychological punishment, to the manipulation and deference of ladies who graciously accept specific roles as proper (the orange section),

2) into a transition where the anger that surfaces propels them to seek less confining ways, bringing them to the conclusion that it is not always others who limit them, but their own learned behaviors (the blue section),

3) and into colleagueship where the mutuality of empowerment is valued (the green section).

Subordinants start the process of change when the pain and burdens of subordinance become intolerable. Those with power over others—the dominants—see no reason to change. Subordination is always confining, and when it is based on gender, race, culture, sexual orientation, class, age, or being differently abled, it is particularly loathsome. Rejection of subordination gives women the power to move first and to create the needed momentum to move women and men along the continuum. The tension of some women moving along this continuum far beyond specific men forces those men to look at themselves in new ways.

It is easy to say that the tension caused by the disparity in timing between women's and men's journeys is necessary for change. Anyone who shares a relationship where this difference exists, however, knows that such tension requires much work for the relationship to stay intact.

With time, as a man moves along the continuum in relation to specific women, he in turn finds himself ahead of other women and men who have yet to leave the confines of role stereotyping. This, too, has its problems.

Subordinant is used here as a parallel to *dominant*. It describes a state, not just a place in relation to a dominant, as the use of *subordinate* would imply, such as in boss/subordinate. Boss/subordinate may or may not include dominance and subordinance.

As both women and men move into the transition and decide that they need to know more about how they interact, learning from their own gender as well as the other, their journeys become more mutually aligned. Their journeys through the transition, though, still have more differences than commonalities. One difference is separating maleness from dominance and femaleness from subordinance.

Heterosexual Model

This continuum describes the journeys of straight men and women in relation to each other. Gay men or lesbians who relate through dominance and subordinance may find much here that is relevant but this book is mainly about straight people's interactions. These reflect worldwide, cultural themes based on heterosexual male dominance and female subordinance (with few exceptions).

Yet, gay and bisexual men often acquire the characteristics of gender dominance for all the reasons straight men do. They are accorded male privilege until they are known to be or perceived to be gay. Their need for invisibility in straight society often supports taking on the characteristics of male dominance. The gay/lesbian community has a long history of lesbians calling attention to the male/female issues which are present. Gay and bisexual men have much to learn from the male/female continuum. Because of their history of cultural subordinance, some gay and bisexual men are sensitive to male/female issues.

We note in this book times when gay male, lesbian, and bisexual experiences differ from straight men's and women's and how a lack of understanding and fear of homosexuality and bisexuality keep straight people from moving on in their gender journey. Because of the lack of visibility of gay men, lesbians, and bisexual people and the dearth of information straight people have about sexual orientation, straight people often treat gay men, lesbians, and bisexual people as if their issues were the same as straight people's.

Straight people's fear of homosexuality and bisexuality is reflected in their gender issues. For a discussion of dominance and subordinance between straight people and gay men, lesbians, and bisexual people, see the companion volume to this book, *Sexual Orientation and Identity: Heterosexual, Lesbian, Gay, and Bisexual Journeys.*[2] Male/female issues and sexual orientation issues are intricately tied together and need to be addressed in a complementary way.

Cultural Contexts

The cultural container which holds the diverse peoples of the United States has its roots in western European culture and Christianity. Each of us, no matter what our cultural heritage, must deal with these European traditions in some way. This is no less true of the way women and men relate to each other than of other aspects of life. Male dominance and female subordinance manifest themselves in nearly all cultural traditions. The behavior patterns described in this book are basically those of the white, western European heritage.

The heart of the Eurocentric tradition is the belief that men have the right to possess and control women. There is a basic deference required of women if they are to be viewed favorably by white men. Whether or not cultural groups, such as those of African, Hispanic, Asian, Middle Eastern, and American Indian* heritage, experience the same specifics of control and deference as described here for white women and white men, all are deeply affected in the United States by the behavior of men and women in the majority white group. In addition, members of diverse cultural groups will want to explore how the traditions of dominance and subordinance are carried out in their day to day lives and whether they have assimilated in a way that assumes the dominant culture's issues. Almost all cultures, if not all, are at some stage of dealing with male dominance and female subordinance. This worldwide theme has many commonalities across cultures. It may be easy for men of color to dismiss this discussion as a western European culture issue. They need to listen to the women of their own culture.

Throughout this text, when we are aware of it, we note if a gender issue has a particular effect on people of color or if a person of color's experience might be significantly different from a white person's. A companion continuum can be found in *Journeys of Race and Culture: Paths to Valuing Diversity*.[3]

As You Read about this Continuum

We assume that everyone grew up doing the best they could, given who they are and the resources available to them. For some people the environment was such that they just survived. Others were nurtured and flourished. Most of us were some place in between. Each generation is a product of its historical time and personal context.

This continuum needs to be read not as an attempt to blame people for who they were and/or are, but as a way to name a process we all share. We hope the insights gained will bring self-understanding that releases us from stuck places, relieves psychic wounds, and expands our world. Accept only what appears to apply to your life, though be aware that what seems unimportant at one time may become relevant at another.

The order of items on the continuum is only suggested. No one fits a schema exactly. What is important is the idea of moving on a journey away from dominance and subordinance through a transition to where power differentials are more equitable.

This volume is structured as a journey along the continuum. Men and dominance is described first, in chapter 2, since male dominance sets the tradi-

---

*We note that many, if not most American Indians have always referred to themselves as American Indian not Native American. Our colleagues who identify as American Indian also note that anyone born in the United States can be considered native American.

tional standard against which all women and men are measured. Women and subordinance are then described in chapter 3. Chapter 4 describes women in transition, since the subordinant moves into the transition first; this is followed by men in transition, chapter 5. Chapter 6 reflects on some important elements of the continuum as we move along our journeys. The vision of colleagueship that we sometimes reach in a few relationships and groups is described in chapter 7. We close with looking ahead from where we are now.

PLEASE NOTE: The Male/Female Continuum graphic is placed at the end of this book so that it can be pulled out for easy reference while reading the text. The words and phrases in dark print in the text denote their use on the continuum.

Men and Dominance

2

Our **entitlement** as men is questioned constantly. Twenty-five years ago the challenge to this power by birthright was dismissed as the work of a few radical feminists of little importance to mainstream life in the United States. Today it is the rare man who is unaware that our dominance over women is in question. Somewhere in most men's personal or work lives, one or more women are pushing them on their assumptions of power. Once-standard male behaviors such as having the final say, moving freely into a woman's space, having one's ideas unconditionally accepted, and expecting to be deferred to are now regularly challenged.

As men raised with the assumption of the gender collusion of dominance and subordinance, our entitlement is well ingrained. Some men have always sought to offset the impact of the collusive system on women and on themselves. Such men have seldom been other than paternal in this effort. Our enmeshment in the dominator culture makes the redefinition called for at societal and personal levels seem enormous. The expectation is compelling and supports us as men and women to find victory in the struggle. It is a personal process that engages us as men to redefine our relationships with women and with other men. It is a societal process that will move us to remake our institutions so that they equitably include all people in their varied diversities.

Gender **entitlement** is only one of the areas of group power by birthright that is being questioned today. Most straight, white men hold an illusion of autonomous individuality while participating in a constant and all-pervasive life-game of who is dominant. Many of us see ourselves as generally subordinate in the male-to-male part of the life-game. Some men choose professions or ways of life that allow them more freedom to be who they are, sidestepping the dominance issue as much as possible. These men, if good at their pursuit, are given special status. The rest are ignored. For instance, men who choose to work as primary school teachers, massage therapists, nurses, secretaries, or in any area that calls for substantial nurturing or anticipating the needs and wants of others are accorded low status by most men. For many men, these others disappear from the screen of manliness for doing such work.

It is a new experience, particularly for white men, to deal with society's attempts at redress for inequities. Some feel that doors are closing to them because of their gender and race. If a straight white man's feelings of entitlement are particularly strong, he may call all action supporting people different from him reverse discrimination. As long as he sees himself and everyone else as an individual and does not acknowledge that he is part of an entitled group that has advantages over people from subordinate groups, he will have difficulty seeing assistance to other groups as anything but unfair to him. He will likely label it reverse discrimination.

Two things may be helpful in relating to the issues of dominance—first, to understand the range of behavior possible between men and women, and second, to think of oneself as on a journey. This continuum puts these together in graphic form.

When moving away from dominance, we have to face who we are if we no longer act dominant over others.* What we have lived and been begin to surface. We face how narrowly defined and destructive our role often is and how many parts of ourselves are deadened by the limiting role of dominance. It is easy to think that letting go of privilege is what is being asked, though the real issue is to move along on a journey to become more whole. The concept that one's life is not just a journey but a developmental journey is not part of "rational" white male culture. Life as a journey toward wholeness is not readily accepted by most men, particularly white Western men. A journey toward wholeness requires untangling the collusion we maintain with women that supports our public dominance and a private and general power imbalance. We are forced to examine our beliefs, inculcated since birth, about what it is to be a man.

For men, dominance is established when as boys we are taught to live without regard for our effect on others and the context we exist in. To discuss the process of a relationship or group with equal regard for all involved seems a waste of time. The result is that male/female relationships are lived as a given, not as a process.

Men who live within the orange section of the continuum expect women to behave in certain ways. We feel comfortable when women function in limited roles—the helping and supportive ones. **Role slotting** women as wife, mother, assistant, helper, care giver, or lover feels comfortable. We are uncomfortable

---

*The pronouns *we* and *us* are used to talk about dominance in the orange part of the continuum because a characteristic of dominants is to individualize themselves and not perceive of themselves as part of a group. It is important that men read this book feeling what it is like to include themselves in this group.

8

with women acting as peer, friend, or colleague. Staying in control is our overriding issue. When women talk about power, it is hard to hear them. If they act nurturing, it is easier. We are used to colluding with women either to act protective or exploitative of them, with the women deferring and accepting their role.

The goal for communicating in the late orange section of the continuum is to be **courteous**, that is, to act the roles of gentleman and lady, not really to understand or know each other. The power differential is covered up with politeness and a demand to adhere to set roles. There is a "rightness" which justifies what happens. The kind of courtesy referred to here is not that of colleagueship, which portrays respect and caring for others, but behavior that confines the woman to role-prescribed responses which let her know she is not entitled to male prerogatives. We speak differently in her presence, withholding certain information and maintaining a calm niceness. This niceness evaporates quickly when the woman tries to go beyond customary roles.

Though we are now acknowledging that many men enter this continuum near the violent end, most men grow up learning to be responsible for and protective of women. White and some other patterns of socialization decree that boys accept a one-up power differential and enter the orange section of the continuum in the **discrimination** and **courtesy** areas. We do not admit that the power differential in this part of the orange section is merely a polite, more subtle version of the physical violence at the beginning of the continuum. Nor is there a vision of a place to go, beyond the power differential of a gentleman and lady. The dominant U.S. culture expects boys to learn to accept themselves as superior to girls and women and other boys and men who are not seen as real men. The often crude ways of showing this superiority, encouraged in the learning process, are expected to be covered up by adult men with gentlemanly behavior, particularly for middle-class people.

Dominance training breeds hostility and contempt toward others considered subordinant. It is foolish and dangerous to vent these feelings on others with our same entitlement. This jockeying among straight (and closeted) men for position over each other leaves us with anger, frustration, and hurt. The resultant hostility of these deadly serious, often covert, dominance games is discharged on those taken for granted as lesser due to their gender, race, sexual orientation, or class. We expect women to take care of our hurts and ignore any pain we inflict on them.

Gentlemanly **paternalism** covers contempt and hostility toward women that is overtly displayed in the orange section. With the niceness of paternalism comes expected deferential behavior, "I will watch out for and take care of you if you will take care of my ego." Proper ways of relating are stressed, and we (men) tend to respect women who stay within the form. The paternalism of white people toward people of color, and those who are financially well off toward those who are not, is similar. There is a deep expectation within paternalism that we (the dominants) will not be made aware of any discontentment with their subordinant status by women or people of color. To do so puts that individual at risk of losing our favor and protection or worse. This shield of seeming protection at a price is not there between heterosexual people and gay men, lesbians, and bisexual people.

The **murder, mutilation, stalking, battering, gay bashing,** and **rape** at the beginning of this continuum are dire expressions of contempt by straight men for women and men who do not fit a manly prescription. Men use **physical violence** and **sexual exploitation** to control women and each other. Women who challenge male entitlement are often considered fair game. Some straight-identified men prey on other men they consider weak to vent their anger and maintain the system. Women and men who challenge or do not support male dominance are especially targeted. They experience both planned assault and arbitrary attack. This actual and potential violence keeps an undercurrent of fear alive for most women and many men.

Sexual exploitation always uses physical intimidation directly or plays on the violence constantly in the background. There is real physical risk, which most straight white men fail to comprehend due to the general safety afforded by our entitlement. The pressure of always needing to be in control, a dynamic of male dominance, keeps most men's sexual exploitation fantasies present or just below the surface. Heterosexual **pornography,** defined by the 1970 Presidential Commission on Obscenity and Pornography as pictures or words that describe sexual behavior characterized by "the degrading and demeaning portrayal of the role and status of the human female," is an integral part of male dominator training.[1] Pornography, and to a considerable degree advertising, inculcates a core value of woman as sex object. We learn to depersonalize women. This depersonalization and the expectation of submission, set in the generally violent environment, lead to considerable hostility being dumped on a woman who does not cooperate in playing out a man's fantasies. This can happen if she refuses to accept sexually loaded comments, declines a sexual invitation, or exercises legitimate power as a manager.

Men commit violent acts such as rape when they feel their life is out of control. Rape is not a sex act. It is an act of violence. It is a way to feel powerful. When the frustration and tension of life in the dominator world seems overwhelming to us as men, we often try to feel in control by exercising authority over women. Terrence Crowley, in his essay "The Lie of Entitlement," speaks for most men when he says, "I don't feel like a man when I'm not in control. I feel confused and vulnerable. It frightens me to say out loud: As long as men control women's bodies, a rape culture will continue. As long as men link sexual excitement with control, domination, and violence, a rape culture will continue. Until the effects of men's behavior on women define the moral value of the behavior, a rape culture will thrive."[2]

The increased presence of women in nontraditional positions that carry authority and the demands for equity in personal relationships make it more and more difficult for us to maintain the illusions necessary to support male entitlement and control over women and seemingly nonmasculine men. The anger, violence, or despair that are often our reaction to the refusal of a special woman to provide expected physical and emotional support may at first surprise us when we encounter this challenge to our seeming birthright. Recognizing the various ways that we demand role behavior and use violence or abandonment to keep a woman in her place are important early awarenesses.

Some heterosexual men believe women have no right to live without them. This belief is reflected in the high rate of nonpayment of court-ordered child support by men in the United States; by the murder, mutilation, beating, and stalking of ex-wives and ex-girlfriends; and by the low rate of prosecution and light sentencing of men for crimes against women. Often when a wife leaves her husband, he simply finds another woman who will give him what he wants and needs because he has been trained to be unable to take care of himself. We get physical and emotional support in exchange for giving a woman security.

Any movement along the continuum in the orange section feels like a gigantic step for us—so much so that it can seem to be a full journey in itself! The man who ceases to physically abuse or **coerce** a woman into sexual relations, moving to the **sexual harassment** of **touching,** verbally **intimidating** such as obscene phone calls, and **teasing,** thinks he has made a major change in his life, and he has. So too does a man who stops **excluding** a woman from those areas of his life involving organization and public power, **avoiding** her presence in order not to have to deal with her. A man who no longer **downplays a woman's presence** in meetings with subtle, or not so subtle, ways of **discounting** or **devaluing** what she says or does (such as avoiding eye contact, reading mail while she talks to him, not building on her ideas, or overly questioning her) thinks he too has changed as much as he can.

Such changes are steps on this continuum, but not what we see as the men's journey. This journey is a process that grows from a choice to join women and other men in creating gender equity. Movement before such an individual choice needs acknowledgment and reinforcement. These changes support opening to colleagueship, even while they are generally made to please women in an attempt to stay connected while maintaining dominance.

Much of our behavior in the discrimination and courtesy areas of the continuum reflects our desire to stay in control and get what we want from women. We tease a woman and make suggestive comments to assert our power and keep the focus on sex or on expected role behavior. When this expectation of being serviced is pointed out to us or resisted by a woman, we make light of the response by saying, "Can't you take a compliment?" "Don't you like being a wife?"—by dismissing the woman in some way. In such exchanges, we assume that if we are comfortable, she should be. We do not see the power imbalance in our expectation of comfort. Farther back on the continuum, resistance to our sexual harassment always had the potential for the assertion of our presumed power through violence. At this stage on the continuum we (men) do not see or understand the repressive power that this threat of violence has over women.

We are taught early and directly that life is rational and indirectly that white, straight men are the guardians of rationality. We learn that anger is a permissible male expression and that it is superior to the many supposedly weaker emotions that are characteristic of women and other subordinants. Moving beyond the collusion of dominance and subordinance and into the transition is not only a rational process, as may be implied by our continuum. To move into the transition requires us opening equally to emotional and rational data. We are pushed beyond expecting everything always to be orderly and precise. It is not easy for us to let go of this assumption of the superiority of the rational over the emotional. As we begin to value more than the quantitative and the rational, we become capable of insight into how we have used being knowledgeable and **all-knowing,** that is, always right—to have the final say with women. As we hear ourselves talking louder when our information is insufficient to hold sway, we are not just learning new ways of relating to women, but new ways of perceiving. We are opening to how we use rationality as a tool for subjugating.

When the process—that is, how things happen—is opened up for discussion, everything ceases to fit into neat pockets and "just is that way." The focus changes from explaining the why of things to living "what is." As we move toward the transition, we may feel that life is switching from being rational to irrational. Actually, it is going from forced rationality and dualistic thinking to diverse ways of perceiving and acting. For we who are steeped in rationality and causality, life can seem out of control at this point.

One of the last acts of men in the orange section is to build barriers between themselves and women by **depersonalizing** them, that is, denying their humanness and individuality by dismissing them as unworthy of attention. There is an undercurrent of anger. It is a last gasp of a dominant attempting to avoid individualizing women and hearing them. Going deeper, it is avoiding dealing with our own behavior and values.

We must open to a journey of self-discovery and personal development if the pain of the gender revolution is to be ameliorated, which we believe most men want and see as best for humanity. Women are claiming their rights to equality and equity with men throughout the world. From culture to culture, these claims are taking different forms, but they join into a steady glacier inexorably moving forward.

This inevitable change opens the possibility of full development for men as well as women. It opens the possibility of connection to ourselves, to other men, and to women. That this capacity is so poorly developed in most of us leaves us only to play a game of dominance over each other. Such behavior supports a dominator society and gives us war and high blood pressure rather than connection with others and with the earth.

The journey for us is first to find what it is to be a man outside of the dominator system, then to engage with other men and women in creating a new way of being.

3 Women and Subordinance

A woman's response to her collusion with men's dominance in the orange section ranges from

— just hanging on, to physical and psychic survival,

— to the power manipulations of the one-down person, who knows how to get her way playing to the inherent weaknesses of one-up people in the **courtesy** section.

No matter where in the orange section of the continuum we are, it is all a matter of survival.* History is full of women who endured their torturers and some who actually murdered them. History also records the women who knew their place and some who refused to accept it.

Mostly, we learn ways to quietly survive from day to day. This **survival behavior** is sometimes referred to as survival mechanisms or victim behavior. Subordinants create ways to cope in order to control their environment and get their needs met. Survival behavior is characte ized by indirect, manipulative ways of getting one's needs met. With so little attention given to women's needs in the orange section, many of us have little or no conscious awareness of them; they include being listened to, developing self-esteem, feeling competent, or having time alone. Even when a need is known, to act on it as valid can be difficult.[1] Women of color, lesbians, older women, women who are differently

---

*We is used in this chapter to facilitate the common bonds of experience as women. If your experience differs, note that and think about how it does and why. Be aware if there comes a time when you see your experience as more similar than you thought.

abled, and women from lower economic classes have to add these life experiences to the one of being a woman, for developing ways to survive. However, some women of color, such as black women, are more assertive about protecting their self-esteem as women. They fight back more in black culture and as a result may be battered less.

A woman's response to men's violence and sexual exploitation at the beginning of the orange section produces violence on her part. Sometimes she explodes to **murder** of an abuser after years of abuse, but usually she is violent and self-destructive toward herself and her children. A woman who lives with battering and rape endures one day at a time. She perceives little hope of surviving by leaving or she would. Acting **helpless** is one way to survive. Her **anger is frozen inside** unless she is provoked over time to her own explosion of violence.

Her efforts to **stay in control** encompass exploding into **physical violence** toward others and **self-destructing** through drugs, alcohol, and suicide. If she can't control or stop the physical violence, her need for control turns explosively inward.

Sustained subordinance in a person's life promotes mental ill-health and **helplessness**. **Suicide** and **addiction**, such as the prevalence of hidden alcoholism among many women, are common reactions. Such self-destructive violence on the part of a woman is not usually seen as a way to try to stay in control of herself and/or a man.

When we are at the violent end of the continuum, we are so concerned with living through each day that any actions or options beyond survival are impossible for us to comprehend. Pointing out that we are at the beginning of a continuum such as this is too painful to handle and to no avail. We need the direct help and support of friends, extended family, co-workers, domestic violence programs, law officials, medical personnel, counselors, and government agencies for dealing with our situation. There is no substitute for such action. Coping with physical violence and sexual harassment are the times in our life when we need protection based on our gender. Otherwise, as an adult person we need to deal with life as it is.

If we choose not to explode with anger because it is unsafe to do so, we can punish a man with psychic violence. We are unresponsive and distant, or we submit without nourishment. If we are forced to live with men's psychic violence of sexual harassment and intimidation, we will likely respond with **enduring, withholding,** and **withdrawing**. These quiet tools—**psychological punishment**—are used by a victim to survive and punish a dominant. Through them we make ourselves psychically unavailable. We withdraw and avoid involvement. As the high incidence of rape, battering, and incest is revealed for women of all ages, all cultures, and all economic levels, the high price of this silence is beginning to be understood.

Though we may wish to get out of such situations, our lack of economic security or our own victimization holds us in these untenable places. Laws, policies, and reporting procedures against abuse and sexual harassment are present for relief. Feeling safe and having enough support to use these tools make the difference as to whether or not we do so. In the 1991 Senate hearings for Clarence Thomas's confirmation to the U.S. Supreme Court Anita Hill showed us the courage it takes to speak and the aftermath we must be ready for if we do. Her testimony described the sexual harassment she experienced from Mr. Thomas ten years before when she worked for him in the federal office of Equal Employment Opportunity of which he was in charge. This office carries responsibility for enforcing the law against sexual harassment. Her testimony was severely questioned and criticized at the time and still is not believed by many. Her character was slandered for speaking out. It became another galvanizing point for women.

It is tempting to resort to feminine manipulations to get our way. Seductive behavior can bring quick results in the short term, but in the long run we may acquire a reputation for being loose or unprofessional. **Seduction** used as a constant manipulative tool is an overt way to control another and survive. Near the beginning of the continuum, our main recourse for expressing power is our ability to give or withhold sexual favors, though sometimes at the cost of physical abuse.

Women of many cultures, but particularly middle-class women and white women, are socialized as young girls to be helpful, **yielding**, and deferential. If we are good and nice, we are rewarded with being liked. Where deference for women is accepted as a cultural imperative, it becomes a basic ingredient of a woman's personality, influencing the way she interacts with men and women, the assumptions she makes about life work, the friendships she develops, and the nature of her spiritual life. In the **manipulation and deference** section of the continuum, our survival depends on how well we have learned to be indirect and invisible. Using deference as a tool means our own needs are secondary to others and usually untended to.

Women from cultures where historically directness in women is assumed and valued, such as African-American and American Indian cultures, are in contrast to women of western European, Asian, and Middle Eastern cultures, where deference is usually a cultural imperative. A Latina's experience is variable. She may not question "the machismo of her man" and therefore finds deference is important, but she may take initiative in many other areas. Even where deference may not be much of an issue in one's own culture, white culture often demands that women of color give deference. A black woman usually finds she is expected to give deference as white women do when working with white men and some non-black men of color, though she is apt to smile less than white women do or some other women of color.

No matter what our culture, it is where we give deference that we develop our need for excessive external approval. Feeling good about ourselves comes to be conditional on how men in general, and also specific men, see us. It gives them the power to define and mold us. Everyone has a need for approval. However, when only certain kinds of people can satisfy our need for approval, it becomes an obsession or habit to satisfy. A constant stream of compliments is expected.

We are open to manipulation by those who would withhold approval according to whether we perform our role well, and who limit approval to those things we do with which they are comfortable. Many women report a constant battle inside themselves over their **excessive need for male approval**. We stay in abusive relationships long after we should leave. Our need for validation is never satisfied as long as it remains in others, not ourselves, particularly others whose self-interest is in staying dominant.

The nature of subordinance produces dysfunctional competition between one-down people: competition for resources, love, approval, and help from dominants. When we rely on a man for our livelihood, we must always make sure that another woman does not take him away.

Such a one-down position makes us excessively reliant on male approval. Men's approval is a basic survival need for subordinant women who learned that deference should be a core trait of the good woman. We constantly ask what we should do and how we are doing. We need a man's response in order to act. Does he really like me better than her? Does this dress look okay? Do I look okay? Should I buy a new car? get a job? find a new one? work for a promotion? Are my marketing ideas worth building on? What should I do with my life? Thinking for ourselves feels not just uncomfortable but a violation of our relationship with a man. We find it difficult to act until a man has affirmed our ideas and planned our actions.

When men relate to us through such roles as mother, care giver, assistant, and lover, we react by **role slotting** them as **husband, brother, boss, father,** and **lover**. We learn to be comfortable with men when they play these roles, and less comfortable with men as peer, friend, and colleague.

To survive by being manipulative and giving deference to men demands learning well how to **bury our anger** for doing this. We are angry at men who put us in this role, about the lost choices for how we would have liked to be, our inability to know who we are and what we could do, the lack of supportive people in our lives, the pretense of being happy when we are not, and most of all at ourselves for playing along. We do not like ourselves, and our lack of self-esteem shows. Our anger leaks out in the most unexpected places.

Where a man specializes in paternalism in the orange portion, a woman becomes adept at **maternalism**. Maternalism and paternalism are both powerful tools for controlling others. Maternalism, as used here, does not symbolize the loving care of mother for child. We express maternalism by trying to control the process of how other adults relate to us and others. We spend much time deciding for others such things as with whom they should be, what to say, and what to expect; above all, we take responsibility for mending their relationships with others. This is our traditional role as a woman. We become the social arranger for everyone and everything. We are responsible for controlling the behavior of men close to us to make it acceptable.

One way in which we do this is by criticizing those men who do not fit the traditional sense of masculinity as strong, athletic, virile, and dominant. We join dominant men in maintaining a narrow sense of what is appropriate male behavior. We punish boys who seem too feminine and sissy, and avoid or gossip about men who are seemingly feminine, sometimes goading on their tormentors.

Some men have difficulty identifying with assumptions of male dominance because inside them is a boy who experienced a dominating, maternalistic mother. These men still may be dealing with her as well as such a wife. Such men know how it feels to live with a woman who, though a subordinant in the world at large, is in full command of the family.

Whether, why, and how much maternalism is expressed varies by culture. A woman of color may adapt such behavior as a protective cover for men who are close to her because of the racism they experience. Black women's role is usually one of being supportive of those she cares about, which often requires her to set aside her own needs. A similar response is true for many Jewish women in response to antisemitism.

Maternalism is tied into a woman's need to **control others by being helpful** in a way that destroys their individuality. She acts as if others are unable to think and act for themselves congruent with their age. Help is extended to those men who perform as they should, that is, take care of us, and is withdrawn when they fail us. The intricacies of relating are based on each person doing the right thing. At the time, this behavior is not called mutual manipulation—at least not openly—but later on as we move into the transition we can acknowledge it for what it is. Maternalism, while a survival tool in the orange section, is self-serving, and in the extreme its perpetrators take on the attributes of martyrdom.

When we move closer to the transition we can look at the meaning of our behavior. As we gain distance from overt violence and have a measure of economic security, we feel safe enough to question what goes on around us. This questioning must take into account the way we collude to support others behaving as they do. It is tempting to blame men for their dominance, but moving into the transition means we own our part in how we have interacted, that is, colluded.

It is not easy to admit that we used and still use manipulation and deference to survive. However painful this admission may be, it must be done because these survival tactics now become a hindrance for moving into the transition. The anger that has been the hidden undercurrent in our life now becomes the driving force to move us into the transition. Without the energy of anger there will likely be no real movement.

Understanding our ways of acting in the orange section as survival behavior is important. It effects our ability to move into the transition. Survival behavior is impossible to give up unless the situation calling for it genuinely changes and we find support for change. Survival behavior cannot be dropped until we are ready to try new ways of acting, which means taking risks. It is also difficult to give up relying on such behavior when so many people, structures, and policies assume that woman's place is to be subordinant. Dominant men and noninclusive organizations make it difficult to stop being a victim or subordinant. Somehow we have to find the safety to move away from the collusion of dominance and subordinance.

As structures become more inclusive and we become more comfortable with ourselves, expanding our networks and support systems, our indirect survival behavior becomes not just useless, it interferes with being a colleague. Breaking our habits of relying on survival behavior is the major work of the transition

Just before we enter the transition, we often waver between **acting** overly **"feminine"** (maybe it will all still work if I'm good enough) and acting out the **anger that is surfacing**. Our anger bubbles up as we become aware of how uncomfortable and unhappy we are with ourselves and everyone around us. This is the anger of all victims for what they have sustained and their rage for the lost parts of their life that can never be recovered. It is owning and talking about our anger that draws us into the transition. Our anger is our ticket to finding the energy for change; it is, of course, what makes people in the orange section uncomfortable and resistant to us and our journey. We are told "women shouldn't be angry."

We are on our journey in the transition.

4 Women in Transition

Women enter the transition for a variety of reasons. Many enter the transition driven by their anger at male dominance. This is especially true for those of us who bought into the norms of dependency for women, such as those that white culture traditionally supports. Some women of color may enter the transition with similar feelings if such things as deference and submission from women have been a central part of their life. For some, entering the transition may primarily involve economic factors of survival. Many women of color are here. For Latinas it may mean proving to oneself and others that it's okay to have standards and expectations of excellence outside the family.

If anger is pushing us, we may be noisy about our entry, though many of us are quiet. We begin to **question everything** that has and does happen to us. We enter a period of full-blown anger, with some women more vocal than others. We tend to **overreact** at the slightest hint our anger is inappropriate. Our behavior varies from demanding to quietly distant and unresponsive. We often drop our feminine ways as a reaction to the confining roles of subordinance.

Our anger at men for all the injustices we now have the courage to express affects how we act. We may suddenly **act "masculine."** We drop stereotypical feminine styles and ways of acting, taking on the characteristics of those we perceive as powerful—men. We cut our hair if long and loose, wear more pants than skirts, and more tailored suits than soft dresses. We stand and walk with an aggressive feel and may swear a bit—or a lot. When straight women take on this new behavior, they are often accused—or fear being accused—of being lesbian.

Though the behavior feels good, it is hard to sustain. We feel guilty about making people uncomfortable and perhaps angry at us. We don't feel nice anymore and may suddenly switch back to acting feminine. We wear high heels and a frilly blouse to work, speak softly (seductively?), and want to know how we can be helpful. We may go back and forth between such extremes of behavior often enough that people become wary of us, wondering who we really are. We probably will decide in time that the overly feminine role feels too manipulative. The strong woman role is more tempting, though scary. It is hard not to **overreact** and be clumsy when trying it out.

Entering the transition is a time of testing. Who am I? Who do I want to be? We feel we have missed out on so much in our acceptance of subordinance. We want to shed the trappings of the orange section. We are energized in a way we have never been.

Where once we may have been a supportive and helpful person, we now may be pushy, aggressive, and highly competitive—fulfilling the worst fears of what a liberated woman is. You may hear us say, "If I'm going to get anywhere, it's got to be no holds barred." We try to **compete indiscriminately,** that is, all-out competition. We are **defensive** if anyone points out what we are doing to ourselves and others—acting like dominants with whom we are so angry. (We may also not do any of the above openly because it isn't safe.) It is almost impossible not to be defensive at this time. Family and friends are likely to try to help by telling us we shouldn't be so angry, in effect pulling us back into orange-section ways. Our partners may complain, argue, threaten to leave, or become violent. Our boss may threaten to fire us. We become quietly defiant and, with good reason, not very trusting.

Our search for our identity, what we really want to do with our life, and how we would like to behave has started. Our defensiveness is a cover for finding space to try out new behavior and ideas, to think for ourselves.

Unfortunately, many women get stuck here, particularly straight women who have relationships of dependency on men. We move into the transition first. Men have not needed to move as long as we were in the orange section. We need the support of other women who are also moving in order to deal with the resistance from men and other women. We will likely be punished for seeming so difficult, different, and unnurturing. This can damage and isolate us, and we may become hardened and avoid connections with others, particularly men.

More and more support is available given the growing number of women moving into the transition. With this support we can be more realistic about what has happened to us and say to ourselves, "The past is the past. My main task is to learn as much about myself as I can and give my time and energy to undoing as best I can what has been done to me. I no longer want to keep my energy tied up in my anger at men." With this we take the giant step forward that will sustain us in the transition. We have made our **decision** that we have much **to learn.** No one—female or male—continues to move through the transition without this commitment.

Though we may repeatedly backslide into seemingly safe, set, traditional roles, we see ourselves on a journey that will bring many changes in us and perhaps in others. The journey becomes personalized. I am the one who needs to change.* I cannot be responsible for other adults. They are on their own journey. I have too much to work on myself. The problem is not just with men. *I have colluded.* What I need to know as a woman is unclear. I have no idea what I want and will spend much time and energy searching for who I am and what I want to do.

A woman socialized to dependency, such as many European-American, Asian, Middle Eastern, and Hispanic women, begins to realize that one of the things that gets in her way is how dependent she makes others on her by always being helpful. **The nature of help needs to change.** It takes too much time. As long as we stay focused on *always* being helpful, we do not learn about ourselves. It is not that we turn away from ever helping anyone again (though it may seem this way to those who have been the receivers of our help). It is just that we can no longer indiscriminately offer help. It keeps us inappropriately maternal. We now say to other adults, "I will help you sometimes because I care about you, as I hope you will help me when I am in need. It is not, however, the basis for our relationship, and I do not want to *have* to help you. It is my choice, *and,* if I choose not to help you, do not punish me for not being the good woman." She learns to say "no" or "later." The African-American woman shares this redefinition of help when she breaks with the obligation to support an African-American man no matter what the costs to her. She too learns the freedom to say "no" or "later."

We now see that in the past, the main way we were allowed to feel powerful was by being in a constant state of helpfulness. It is easy to feel as if power is slipping away when giving up what has been our main purpose in life, to always be helpful. It is hard to let go of this kind of power because it has been our main way for feeling loved and appreciated.

One of the most difficult things to let go of is giving help and advice to men about their journey. We assume their journey should be identical to ours, and of course it is not. In many cultures, one of straight women's main tasks in the orange section is taking care of men's emotional life and their relationships. He "lets" us be the expert. Therefore, we will probably act as if what we did to enter and move into the transition is what a man "should" do. In our haste and excitement for a man to experience freedom from dominance (we have a high stake in this), it is tempting to equate his journey with ours. "If I had to learn thus and so, then that must be what he must learn."

The resistance that springs from men when we try to help them with their journey is immediate and real. We can use men's resistance to facilitate letting go

---

*The use of *we* in the transition is important in establishing our common journey. The use of *I* is also important. We each make this journey for ourselves. I need to own my part and speak for myself. The reader is encouraged to read *we* as I for herself.

of outdated ways for surviving and feeling powerful, and for gaining space to have more time for our own journey. Both women and men need space from the other gender to do what is relevant for their movement toward colleagueship.

Just as men in the transition need to pay special attention to their relationships with other men, heterosexual women, who have had cultural affirmation to be dependent on men, need to attend to their relationships with other women. In doing this we face the issue of the undercurrent of **competition** that is present **between women** in the orange section. Straight women with excessive need for male approval in the orange section support inherent competition with other women. Destructive competition between women takes the form of gossip, power struggles, and the need to push other women down, that is, to do them in. Sometimes competition is more subtle—we just avoid engaging with other women. We may say we prefer men's company. If we spent more time with boys growing up, we may be more comfortable around boys and men, especially if they seem to do more exciting things.

The question becomes, If I am uncomfortable with women generally or in specific relationships or groups, what am I missing in affirmation, support, and understanding of myself as a woman? As straight women lessen their usually unconscious competition with other women and create supportive networks, their **search for excessive male approval lessens** and connections with other women expand.

Straight women need to be more thoughtful about their relationships with other women, as lesbians often are. We sometimes think because we have one or two close friendships that we have no issues of competition between women. As straight women in the orange section, we don't think about the amount of time and energy given to men, the focus of our sexual energy. We don't consider the effect on our relationships with women when we talk incessantly about men. There is a lack of balance between our friendships with women and with men. We block out or give little attention to women's friendships that would focus on our needs and lives as women. This behavior is a holdover from role stereotyping. The transition is a time to bring balance into our lives.

Lesbians usually have more freedom from the high need for approval from men, because they are not emotionally dependent on men in the way straight women are. Straight women often find lesbian friends can be a welcome relief from other women friends whose life is geared constantly to pleasing and competing for male attention. Lesbians and straight women in the transition may give us affirmation and support for our own needs and intuition, if we have taken the time to build trusting friendships.

Trusting relationships between straight women and lesbians have not been the norm. White heterosexual women in the orange and early blue sections often punish lesbians, women of color, and other straight women who are further along on this continuum for being powerful. They are thought to be bad women who mess up men by matching men's strength and authority, and give no deference.

One straight female secretary left a note on her computer when she quit, refer- ring to her suspected lesbian boss as one of those superbitch females.

Lesbians may also have issues of competition with straight women and other lesbians. For instance, some lesbians have an overwhelming need that all women agree on important issues and act alike. The anger at disempowered sta- tus leads to an intolerance of diversity among women and a one-right-way men- tality. This promotes competition for being the one who sets the standard for what the agreement will be and what the proper way to act is.

Support systems, feedback, networking, mentoring, and giving consistent reliable time to friendships with straight women and lesbians of all races and cultures are part of learning about and taking care of ourselves. As we change our image of power from control of others and things to one of cooperating, facilitating, and sharing power, the automatic competition with other women is reduced or eliminated. We begin to appreciate our need for colleagues, both women and men, who respect and appreciate this different sense of power.

Some women have more cultural affirmation for being powerful, direct, and assertive than others do. Many women of color are accorded authority with- in their culture, but not in white society. They experience the discord of moving between the esteem of family and friends and the expectation that they will defer when entering the white world to work. Some women of color, especially black women, carry an expectation from others of strength and power, particu- larly when faced with adversity. This stereotype can be a tiresome one to fulfill. The possibility for being oneself naturally—both someone with strength, but also someone able to be vulnerable and relaxed at times—is difficult. Those who are ascribed such characteristics as strength usually find it a setup in that others take advantage of them; after all, "they can take anything, they're strong."

For those without cultural affirmation, the ways a woman experiences being powerful begin to change in the transition. We grow more comfortable with power, though for awhile we give mixed messages—sometimes drawing power to us and other times pushing it away. It is clear we want neither to con- tinue the manipulative power of the victim nor copy how power is handled and acted out by dominants. We look for ways other people show strength, influ- ence, and power as well as look for different experiences and models in our own histories.

As we live in this inclusive sense of power, our feelings of self-empower- ment grow in direct proportion to the decline in our need for excessive male approval. By sharing our experiences with other women, we redefine power for ourselves in a way that perceives it as expanding, like love. When others are empowered, our power expands. We learn we can **acknowledge** the **power** we have and enjoy it. We stop using power to oppress or manipulate.

It is here that the overarching transition work of **building self-esteem** starts to become evident. For some of us—for instance, many white and Asian women—building self-esteem is crucial. For black women, lack of self-esteem is not a problem so much based on gender in black culture than one based on the effects of racism in white culture. Issues of self-esteem vary for Latinas. For those who have arrived more recently in the United States, deference may be more of a cultural imperative than for those who have lived in the United States a generation or more. Many Latinas have developed their self-esteem within the home, where women are often seen as powerful. As women in our myriad diversities, we begin to have insight into how we do or do not participate in oppression as subordinants to sustain male dominance.

Redefining power causes women socialized to dependency to think through what it means to be perceived as aggressive. We are aware of the many men who avoid us or are unresponsive when we become direct or show authority. We need to be clear that to be assertive means being direct and competent. This is not aggression. Aggression has an edge of anger, hostility, and/or contempt. It is getting one's way without consideration for others. Holding assertiveness as an exchange between equals is difficult with a man who sees women as subordinate. He sees any direct action by a woman as a challenge to his entitlement. **Lesbian baiting**, that is, using derogatory names and harassment to dismiss women as lesbians, whether they are lesbian or straight, is one way some men try to avoid dealing with women who show authority.

The narrow boundaries for assumed deference in the orange section now feel too binding. Most of us need to learn that it is all right to be much more assertive than we are used to being. We frequently think we are aggressive when we are really only assertive. If we were socialized to dependency, to stand out in any way can seem to us overbearing. We need to get used to feeling empowered and direct. As we **increasingly** become **assertive**, others may be uncomfortable at first and need time to get used to the "new" us. Because many perceive a woman as aggressive when she shows any strength or leadership, we need to find others whom we trust to give us feedback on when we are assertive and when we have stepped over into aggression.

Many women of color, who are supported for assertiveness within their culture, are thought to be hostile and aggressive in white culture where racism is present. White people in the orange section tend to punish assertive women of color by undermining and avoiding them or expecting them to be overly competent. White women are often patronizing and unsupportive, isolating them in women's groups. Assertive women are found in all cultures. White women, in particular, need to pay attention to whether they recognize and value the resources assertive women of color bring to groups and organizations. We have a poor track record culturally for doing this. It is important to be comfortable with assertive women of color, sometimes matching their energy without competing for attention. Women need to look cross-culturally, as well as within the lesbian community and their own culture, for role models of assertive women. Understanding the different ways assertiveness and aggressiveness are viewed and supported in different cultures is important in order to be inclusive of all women.

As we move through the transition, our awareness grows for how we have interacted with or avoided lesbians, gay men, and bisexual people. Our emotional reactions to homosexuality and bisexuality are likely closer to the surface. **Addressing our homophobia and biphobia** has increased in importance. It is impossible to deal with gender issues without including issues of sexual orientation. For one thing, so much of the gender journey involves straight women wanting straight men to change, that is, to become more sensitive and process-oriented. Until we deal with our homophobia we will likely give mixed messages to men about such changes. We will say how we would like men to change, but when they do, we have an emotional reaction of discomfort. They don't seem masculine enough. This reaction is often tied up in our discomfort with men who seem soft or gentle. We often experience these men as effeminate, that is, stereotypically gay, even though many gay men do not have such characteristics nor are they as sensitive as we would like them to be. Straight women as well as men need consciously to expand the range of male behavior with which they are at ease.

The importance of being inclusive of all men and women has been mentioned throughout the orange and blue sections. For straight women, lesbians are our allies in understanding women's journey away from subordinance. They often see the issues more clearly because they are not partnered with men. We need their support on our journey as they need ours.

Whereas a man needs to spend time developing introspection, a woman in the transition who was socialized to deference needs to become aware of the excessive time spent inside herself thinking about how things are rather than initiating and doing. In the past, little girls were more apt to learn to be quiet and read than to compete and develop large motor skills. When girls are expected to be nice and not question what others tell them to do, they retreat inside themselves, developing an active fantasy life.

Though much is changing, many women were socialized in this way. This socialization encouraged us to think about process more than to act on it: we became observers rather than doers. It is tempting to try to control the world "by thinking things through" rather than getting out there and experimenting. Our active internal thought processes often freeze our behavior. We perceive so many options and possibilities in a situation that as a result, we do nothing. Women see the context of information, which is a useful skill in collegial relationships. However, such **introspection must not freeze our actions.** We must not get so far into data overload that we do not make decisions and act.

As we move closer to colleagueship, we look at our anger from one more perspective. If we were trained to feel guilty for being angry, such guilt has been an undercurrent as we moved through the transition. We remember how easily we were dismissed in the orange section for being unladylike and unacceptable because we got angry. Just when we think it no longer holds us in its grip, our anger seems to rear up again. We hope our anger has changed from the overriding presence it was in the early transition to a source of energy that sustains us on our journey (there is no going back). Anger is a healthy emotion when it is expressed in the moment and not bottled up. If we still experience anger as a deep well of personal rage, often unfocused at everyone and everything, we may need good friends who will hear us out or, in some cases, professional help. It is difficult to be a friendly, nonjudgmental partner or colleague with anger leaking out much of the time.

By the end of the transition, both men and women have learned a great deal about **differentiating people**—waiting to get to know them before assuming what they like and dislike and how they will act in a variety of situations. In the collusion of dominance and subordinance, our first reaction was to look for commonalities among people in a group. If we didn't find them, we usually assumed them, projecting onto others what we wanted to see in them. Another way to meet people or enter groups is to assume diversity will be present and to feel excited about how that will emerge—being surprised at commonalities, not diversity. Diversity is rarely acknowledged or honored when our first reactions are to latch onto commonalities with others rather than acknowledge and appreciate the differing experiences that come from our gender, race, culture, sexual orientation, class, physical abilities, and age.

Dominance and subordinance demand that differences be covered up. Even minor differences make us uncomfortable and unsure how to act. Friendship and mutual regard seem out of the question. In colleagueship, such differences do not automatically preclude friendships. Compatible value systems that appreciate diversity are what matter now.

It is in building connections with other women who are of differing races, cultures, sexual identities, classes, physical abilities, and ages that the ground work is laid for **building women's institutions.** A major way dominants maintain their power over others is to create institutions and patterns of behavior that keep subordinants separate from each other and devalue the diversity among them.

In order for women as a group to never again revert to subordinance, it is important that time and effort be given to creating and maintaining supportive women's institutions. Institutions that move us out of the orange section are domestic violence and rape crisis centers, women's health centers, and groups that support legal redress for discrimination of all kinds. We need to support the political organizations that have fought for these services and given us choices in life. We also need to build those that create new models for partnership and inclusion across race, culture, sexual orientation, class, age, and differing abilities. Clear **identification with diverse women's communities** is basic to sustaining the support systems and networks needed to move women and men into colleagueship.

Men in Transition

5

Leaving dominance is disorienting. Anxiety, fear, pain, and alienation from given ways of acting and being press in on us. Irrational **anger surfaces** for no obvious reason. We are moving into a transition that will reshape how we see and live out gender in the world and in ourselves. Seemingly little things, such as a woman refusing to defer, complaining of the way she is touched, or saying no when we try to be helpful, can be a disaster.

Entering the transition is confusing. We acknowledge privately that women are not always treated the way they should be, and we would not want to be treated as some are. We work hard to say the right thing and be knowledgeable about what is good for women. We try to be politically correct.

Still operating from the mind-set of dominance, we seek to learn new ways to treat women. That one woman wants one thing and another wants something else seems intentionally complicating. Why can't they agree? We often place or project our confusion and anger onto women. We see women confused about what they want. We amplify their anger and take it personally. We do not see or accept the confusion, anger, and defensiveness that is ours. Confusion and anger spring from not knowing how to respond to a woman who demands equity and stops fitting herself into a stereotype to help us be comfortable.

We have good intentions and focus on saying, and in tentative ways doing, the right thing. We try to hear in a new way a woman who points Out something that is offensive about our behavior. We hear our **defensiveness** in response to feedback that our behavior is not in line with our words. As a prelude to change we begin to see how our desire to know how to act before we

27

interact with women is a trap of dominance. We are learning that good intentions are not enough. The impact of our behavior counts as much or more than our intentions. Here is an area where men whose traditions have not supported awareness of the relationship of words and behavior can learn from men who have. For example, African-American men have a keen sense, honed from coping with white racism, of the consistency or inconsistency of words and behavior. Black men are generally less defensive when women are assertive or aggressive. They are used to relating to black women who have a considerable history of assertive behavior in gender relationships.

We are not accustomed to individualizing women. We may separate out those who are special to us in traditional roles, but we set limits on women outside such roles. When we have to deal with a woman who does not fit our stereotype, a common reaction is, "How dare she change the game plan of the ways men and women are supposed to relate?" These rules are deep within us. Shame, intimidation, and sometimes physical force undergird this basic socialization. As boys it was not easy to learn to let girls go first or to figure out that they were either special or "the other kind of girl."

Learning that much of what we do as gentlemen is a cover for dominance is hard. Early in the transition we want to focus on the hurt and pain of how we learned, not the privilege of entitlement. We want to respond to the needs of women in ways that keep them dependent. It is difficult for us to see how we limit women finding out in their own way what they can do. As long as we take the screwdriver out of a woman's hand when we think she needs help or insist on **acting knowledgeable** even when we know less, we are not giving her the room needed to find, let alone demonstrate, her ability. We also never have to face that she may be more competent in an area we consider ours. When we continue such behavior with a woman seeking a sense of herself and her abilities, she is forced to distance herself from us in order to explore more fully her competencies. Some of us catch on early and change our ways in the interest of maintaining a relationship. Some of us don't get the point until after our fourth partner leaves us or a sexual harassment charge is made.

Women who question male dominance tap anger that is deeply rooted in us. Two important sources of our anger in the beginning of the transition are

— the control and manipulation women exert on us as part of the collusion that maintains our dominance, and

— the ways the cloak of dominance has co-opted us to accept personally that we are far less than we are.

These sources of anger, which only gradually become clear, are also sources of grief and a sense of fundamental loss. We accept our complicity in the lie and the rip off that demanded we deaden, bury, and deny large parts of who we are in order to be "real men." We were cheated out of a full, healthy experience of life through buying into dominance.

The overt anger we have shown throughout the orange section needs to be distinguished from the anger in the early blue section. Anger in the orange section is controlled and controlling, and never aimed at ourselves. There is an edge of violence to it even in its most benign forms. Women tell us that it feels both set and abrupt, and the impact results in ridicule and dismissal of them. In the transition our anger is more reactionary and, to us, surprising as to when it pops out. It is multidirectional and mixed with grieving and loss. We use anger to get space, to establish boundaries for psychological safety, to punish women for their part in our socialization, to cover hurt feelings, and at times to reestablish the old order, even if it is no longer wanted.

We are likely to alternate between defensiveness and charm, hurt and arrogance, caring and distancing. We work hard to be seen as put together when much of the time we feel as if the known world has vanished and we are making everything up as we go and doing it alone. No one, particularly another man, is going to get a glimpse of the inconsistent and emotionally driven creature we feel we have become. We try to sound as if we know clearly what we are talking about on every topic. Women who push us on our need to control are **defeminized** by us as hard and overly competitive. No matter how a strong woman presents herself, we see in her only the reflection of our own anger. Seeing her as an angry, hostile bitch is a reflection of how we have behaved.

When defeminizing is an issue for African-American and American Indian men, it is mainly a reflection of the Eurocentric tradition. To be female in these traditions has not been to be dependent. Coy, self-differentiated behavior toward men by women has not been cultivated in these more gender-equitable cultures.

In the workplace we **compete indiscriminately** with any woman who exhibits anger or even a level of directness. "If she wants to be equal, have it all, be one of the boys, then she will damn well have to take care of herself!" "You don't want to be protected?—fine, then may the best man [sic] win!"

As painful a time as this is, some form of overreaction probably is needed. It is only by feeling the full force of our anger that energy for change becomes available. One cue that we have moved into the transition occurs when we break out of the gentleman's stance of feeling guilty about showing anger to a woman.

We start the transition with a need to identify with the anger inside of us and our desire to punish women—all women—for changing the rules of the game. We have a strong need to push away from women. Sooner or later most men come to the conclusion that feeling angry and alone is not what life is all about. At some point, and in some way, each man needs **to decide** for himself **that he has much to learn** and that **he is on a developmental journey.**

This is the clear turning point on the continuum for us. With this decision there is no going back. We decide to be a part of creating what is to be.

With this decision to learn, the quality of the movement along the continuum changes. Our focus turns to what was lost because of assumptions of dominance and the quality of our relationships with both women and men. We view what happens around us as data to be looked at, thought about, and talked about with others. We work to stop passing judgment on the meaning of what others do and work more on understanding the implications for a shared relationship and how it changes us.

We become more direct with women. It feels harsh and discourteous at first. It is hard to respond to a woman's offer of warmth and caring if it feels at all manipulative. We question our perceptions, we make mistakes, and we are inconsistent in our interactions. Staying centered in our development gets hard when a woman important to us demands attention and we are not in a place to give it to her. Formerly, we would have faked a response. Now our desire is for authenticity in relationships. We try to release ourselves from the grip of chivalry which keeps us from direct interaction. We feel vulnerable, clumsy, but also we sense a new potential for connectedness. So that this part of our transition is not a disaster for our relationships, we must share what we are doing. Talking with women who are important to us about what we are thinking, feeling, and trying to do begins the work of creating a new relationship outside the dominator paradigm.

In the orange section of the continuum we generally paid little attention to women and what they said unless we wanted something from them. Here we learn to ask questions and pay attention to their responses. **Listening** more fully, resisting our impulses to give our opinion or be knowledgeable, changes what is said to us and increases choices. The focus of the interaction is off of us and on what the woman is saying. With this shift, a major barrier to male/female colleagueship falls.

Asking questions as part of developing good listening skills with women is harder than it seems at first. Staying engaged, having flexibility in the type of questions we ask, not using questions as opportunities to make statements, and not doing most of the talking are important for good listening—though not the way we usually have acted. It is often surprising that, when we first try to be more focused on listening to women, we end up doing most of the talking. The difference is that now we observe ourselves doing so and can gather data on our behavior and try again.

About here anger, helplessness, and confusion often press in. We want to give up and return to what we know, yet we can't. Finding a woman we can listen to, hearing what she says, and thinking about what she tells us can be extremely helpful.

In **learning to be direct and nonprotective** of women, we grapple with our paternalistic ways of keeping women dependent and distant. Saying directly what we think and feel, giving descriptive feedback, and being fully present changes power balances. In the orange section we held a narrow view of what women can do well. We treated women who showed propensities beyond those areas as an exception. Now we see connections between opening doors and other things we do for a woman, and our expectations that she will defer to us. We hear violence toward women in some of today's music as an attempt to assure that women know their place in a man's world. We see the dysfunction of putting women on a pedestal if we are to relate as equals. We also accept that we took women off the pedestal when they did not conform to our expectations. This change to a more equitable way of relating takes time and dialogue.

In the orange section, helping a woman affirmed to us that we were better at or more knowledgeable about something than she was. It helped us feel in charge. Our usual response to a request for help from a woman was to think her incompetent and to take over. **As the nature of our help changes,** we see that when a woman requests help she is seldom asking us to take over. As we explore various ways of assisting and fitting our help to the particular situation, we learn that our need to fix things for women was another way of keeping them dependent. We come to see that a request for assistance may be the opening of a dialogue in which both of us may learn. If we are managers, we may have to be direct about our limits for being helpful. We did not have to deal with these limits when we simply took over problems rather than engaging a woman in dialogue about help appropriate to the situation. Being interactive rather than acting for a woman pushes us. We see how we have equated maleness and dominance when helping women. We now understand a woman when she says, "When you take over a problem and fix it, you stop communication and take on work you needn't."

As men we have kept alive an illusion of independence and self-sufficiency through a complicated dependence on one or a few women. We go out each day to struggle with other men and a few women in the marketplace of life with the sense that we go alone, emotionally self-sufficient.

Traditional men may sometimes be vulnerable with special women in their lives: mother, wife, lover, and, to a lesser extent, women in secretarial and other supportive jobs. As long as a woman attends to us and helps us feel connected and affirmed, we accord that woman special status, financial support, and protection.

Observing the day-to-day world of men in the orange section, we easily conclude that many of us simply do not like women. Why else the violence and hostility? What is it we carry as men that so confuses love and abuse, and caring and control? Scratch the surface of anger and we find fear. But fear of what? That is where the confusion runs deep. We do not talk about fear and especially fear of women. We fear that which consciously and unconsciously we know can hurt or control us. As men we need to acknowledge and explore the degree to which we are **emotionally dependent on women.** We do not speak here of the healthy interdependence of a man and woman who love and care about each other, but of those who blindly follow prescribed roles for men and women.

Many of us have been coerced to suppress our feelings of grief, resentment, anger, fear, and joy since we were preschoolers. This is well documented as the experience of the majority of white men and some men of color. What we don't discuss is how we have come to depend on the women in our lives (personally and professionally) to monitor, rearrange, and inform us about our feelings. We often need someone to tell us what we feel, but they must do it in a manner that does not threaten us. A substantial number of straight men will say, "My wife is my best friend." The second part is, "My wife is my only real friend." If a woman seeks to change her relationship to us or to explore directly with us the depth of her dependence, our desperation at being left alone creates fear and anger, and we simply act out in a controlling manner to protect the status quo.

Our paternalism hinders us from dealing with our ingrained fear of being left alone. Being responsible is implicit in this collusive pact of the orange section. This pact stipulates that "you protect me from my fears of inadequacy as a man and I will protect you from external harm and provide economic security." We take responsibility, RESPONSIBILITY, **RESPONSIBILITY** for her. It starts in childhood. Many of us as young boys are inappropriately put in situations where we feel responsibility for others. The messages about being in charge, providing, and protecting women get connected to our definition of manhood before we have had a childhood. There is much pressure in our society to create "little men." Boys feel overwhelmed, fearful, and inadequate when they cannot fulfill these impossible expectations. Feelings of inadequacy get buried and held deeply. Large numbers of us pursue such things as responsibility, control, and achievement with an obsession that is ultimately exhausting. We never can be "man enough." These feelings are carried as a constant, low-level resentment toward women who are likely viewed as not having to make it. If they make it, fine, but if they don't they are still women. These feelings of "never enough" cause men to experience deep isolation. How can a man say, "I don't feel adequate"?

It is important to emphasize how much more complex this situation is for men of color. The dominant (straight, white, male) culture says to all men, "Part of being a man is taking care of yourself and of women important to you." To some men of color it says, "If you can get work at all, expect to be rewarded less than white people and know that you stand up for women or yourself at considerable risk." It says, "Man of color, if you play by white rules and give us no static about it, expect modest reward. If you help maintain the system by criticizing other people of color who speak for needed change, we will give you special recognition. If you can make a major contribution we will see you as an exception. And by the way, if you will entertain us and act as if the rewards of the system are available to any individual willing to work hard, we will pay you big dollars. Be sure to remember that lesser whites, men in particular, are given the right to remind you of your powerlessness when those of us who are privileged are not around to protect you."

Most white people assume too often that people of color have to confront the same issues as they do. This assumption stops the listening we need to do to hear where there are similarities and differences. Of even greater impact is our tendency as dominants to project our fears and the things we do not like about ourselves onto those we consider subordinant. This behavior makes us dangerous to people of color. It also helps us avoid addressing our fears of dependence on those we consider subordinant or examining how our self-identity is tied to our dominance over others. We do not mean that the issues raised here are not real for some men of color, but as white men we must not assume that systemic white male issues apply to men of color.

As we move away from dominance, the fundamental issue of our identity arises. Who am I outside of dominance? becomes a vital question for those of us who identify as straight white men. How we have lived and who we have been begin to be visible to us. We begin to see how narrow and confining our societally prescribed roles are. We begin to see how destructive we are individually and collectively in living our assumed entitlement. We sense how much of ourselves we have deadened in pursuit of the ever-elusive true manhood.

Up to this point, as straight men we have paid much attention to our interactions with and feelings toward women. About this place on the continuum our **connections with other men** are legitimized for exploration. These connections have been based in sports activities, intellectual exchange, or the workplace. Now feeling alone and not understood by women important to our lives, we open up and talk to other men about what is happening to us. Talking about the stresses and joys of everyday life becomes important. Those of us who are straight become aware of how dependent we are on women for the quality of our emotional life. We see how we gave the development of significant parts of ourselves to women. The central work of the transition for us, reforming connections with other men and taking charge of our emotions, has begun.

In order to do our own learning, we may need to gain some distance from women for awhile, particularly those closest to us. We need to step back to gain perspective on what goes on around us and how we unconsciously fit in. We also need to find other men who are ready to do the same so that we can support each other on our journeys. The behavior and image of a loner, maintained to ensure the respect of other straight white men, is no longer possible without the support of women.

We begin to take time to become aware of how undeveloped our introspective and spiritual lives are. Our sense of spirituality often has lain dormant; if we have given it attention, it too has often been built on a spiritual hierarchy of men being more important than women and therefore closer to God. We talk about how unconnected men are abusive to women and each other, and how they create an abusive culture. Competition and homophobia, which underlie our male friendships, now interfere with what we need to do. Time spent with a few other men who have identified with the journey away from dominance becomes precious. It becomes clear that it is not just with women that we will progress toward colleagueship, but with other men as well. We learn that the women's journey is not our journey and that our journey has its own excitement, pain, challenges, and rewards.

We need to be introduced to the ever-increasing volume of literature, film, art, and spiritual and human growth experiences that show men have a developmental journey. We come to know that it is possible to transcend a narrow definition of manhood and become richer and deeper human beings. We don't just grow up, get a job, get partnered, have children, climb a ladder, retire, and play golf. We see that there are large numbers of men in every profession and calling today who are consciously seeking a journey. Our journey is **increasingly introspective** and spiritual.

Coupled with an inordinate emotional dependency on women, we (most straight and some gay men) carry a substantial fear of intimacy with other men. We often avoid even superficial discussion with other men about what troubles us. Part of this fear is about competition, but much of it is simply fear of getting close. When we as heterosexual men are drawn close to another man, feelings of caring and affection arise; then, **homophobia** asserts itself. We have been taught to distrust and disavow any feelings of closeness with other men which are not based in sports, combat, business, or intellectual activity. As straight men we fear that other men will misunderstand our intentions or think we are homosexual. As a result, much of our censoring of relationships with other men is unconscious and happens before we are even aware that fear is managing the quality of our relationships.[1]

Homophobia, even when it is no longer an absolute blocker, is a constant governor on the development of male/male relationships. Distrust of male-to-male relational intimacy is also experienced by some gay men, who are sexual with one another but find friendship or sustained intimacy much more difficult. We see that trust, affection, and vulnerability between men are tied to how we maintain the dominator system with each other. We believe that intimacy with each other or with women can only be developed as we join the struggle to create a new system. The equating of sex and intimacy confuses and helps maintain homophobia as a destructive force. As we seek each other out to learn to grow beyond our socialized separation, homophobia and heterosexism are center stage.

Men's fear of other men goes beyond fear of intimacy. It leads them to leave unchallenged the abusive behavior of men toward men as well as women. The ascribed male characteristics of being direct and confrontive are quite limited. We use directness when talking about ideas, ball teams, and information: we use confrontation to show who has dominance over others. Neither is used in dealing with others' behavior, attitudes, or core values. In fact, it is rare that, as men, we confront one another about behavior or attitudes. Our direct, confrontive, and aggressive behaviors, so evident among us when we discuss ideas and exchange information, are seldom used to challenge the existing order. We know to keep our behavior supportive and our attitudes and core values to ourselves if they do not fit with those who have power over us.

When a man calls another man on his behavior in public, the issues of male-to-male dominance surface. Power differences maintained through private sanctions are questioned. Such challenges, particularly in front of women, a subordinant group, raise the issue of "face." The unspeakable is said; retribution or a change in the power relationship is necessitated. To challenge another man's behavior in support of a subordinant group such as women questions the system. The most common sanction for such a challenge is to be shunned and placed outside the male order. Our self-worth in the orange and well into the green section is based on unexamined assumptions and well-practiced male-to-male behavior that supports superiority over each other. We collude to keep both the reality and the illusions of dominance as they are. It is not until we find support with other men in the transition that we can see beyond the notion that a man is nothing if he is not in control of something or someone, that is, keeps **centrality**. Dominant people have a way of keeping themselves central to whatever happens. Keeping centrality means the focus is always on us, no matter where we are or what we are doing.

As we near the end of the transition, we are ready to **deal with men in the orange section**, breaking the code of silence on their behavior. As we do this we give relief to women who have carried the burden of taking on men and their behavior. As we do this we experience the same discounting, anger, and hostility that women do as they address orange-section behavior with men.

Standing firm yet flexible in confronting dominant behavior in other men is a major challenge. Going neither one up nor one down with other men requires skill and centeredness when one is challenged, as is the dominator way. This challenge may come from a man who sees us as another dominant trying to establish his way as the way or who sees us as having sold out and not worth listening to. Men who are not ready or willing to dialogue may be dangerous to us personally as well as opposed to gender equity. Because of our new vulnerability we must learn to pay attention to our safety and that of our colleagues in ways we may never before have considered.

We are now ready to talk with and strategize with willing women and men about creating an environment to foster colleagueship. Our strategies include ways to keep people in the orange section from destroying what we are creating, out of their fear of and defensiveness about something they cannot yet grasp other than as a threat to how they live their lives.

Reflections on the Continuum So Far

As we move along our journeys, the transition has laid the groundwork for communicating our perceptions of the processes and relationships we share with those of the same and the other gender. We find that how things happen is as important as what happens. Before moving on to chapter 7 on colleagueship, several areas of concern need special attention. They are:

— what makes us move along a continuum such as this;

— how we cycle back and forth through the continuum;

— how people of color relate to the continuum;

— how gay, lesbian, and bisexual people relate to the continuum;

— how we deal with nontransitional people, that is, women with nontransitional men and men with nontransitional women;

— how women and men interact in organizations; and

— how diverse groups avoid competition.

What Makes Us Move Along This Continuum

Why would anyone want to move along this continuum if it requires so much time, energy, and discomfort? It seems safer to stay in the courtesy part of the orange section. We would avoid resistant and angry reactions from others (spouse, boss, lover). If we have the luxury of asking why move, we probably will stay where we are, at least for the moment. We simply are not pressed enough by circumstances around us.

As stated in the preface, this book is not intended to prescribe what we should be doing. Rather, it describes how many are acting because of their inner needs, pain, and anger, usually in response to others.

We move along the continuum for a variety of reasons.

— Others whom we care about force us to look at ourselves differently.

— Our second (third, fourth) attempt at partnership or marriage doesn't seem to be working any better than our first. We are almost ready to give up on commitment.

— At work teamwork and colleagueship are assumed by our boss and co-workers. Our job depends on it.

— We cannot get what we want out of life without moving into the transition. The pain is too great to stay where we are. The unfulfilled energy and longing for a different way to be and relate to others are overwhelming.

— Our emotional and physical health depend on doing the work of the transition. The stress of remaining either dominant or subordinant is too great. Taking another aspirin, running an extra mile, changing our diet again, or working fewer hours doesn't take care of the stress we feel.

— Our spiritual growth demands an authentic, intentional life of equitable relationships and groups.

— We know we will never learn about and appreciate our unique way of perceiving the world and ourselves, as long as we accommodate to dominance and subordinance.

— Et cetera (in other words, add your own).

Since we live in a democracy, individual people have a right to be wherever they are on the continuum—which means not moving (as long as they do not violate the civil and criminal law) as well as moving. When there is hope and support or when life becomes untenable where we are, we start moving.

Cycling Back and Forth through the Continuum

No one moves through this continuum in a step-by-step, linear mode. We constantly cycle back and forth, depending on what day it is, how we are feeling, where we are, and with whom. Some days we feel just great and seem to be moving along; other days things happen which push us back into our anger. Sometimes we find we defer more or fight back more than we are aware of at the time, or we act maternal or paternal at times when we thought we never would again. We change by rushing in, cycling back and forth, entering a plateau to consolidate for awhile—never by straightforward movement through the continuum. Sometimes we need rest periods.

Realistically, given the society and our socialization, we do not leave completely the orange part of the continuum (except, hopefully, the early violent part) but rather add more places to be, along with acquiring skills and the support of others to deal with those still living in the orange section. We have lived too long with dominance and subordinance, and are still in a culture embedded in it. What we can expect is, first, gradually to center ourselves beyond the collusion of role stereotyping and well into the transition beyond the **decision to learn,** so that we are aware when we move back on the continuum. Then we can assume a stance of cycling between the transition and pushing into colleagueship—with relapses back to role stereotyping at times.

Some of this movement back and forth can be viewed as part of the cycle of learning, with developmental regression and times for consolidation and integration of new information. Part is in reaction to others and to circumstances that require or stimulate old behavior. Much of the seeming movement is simply our attempts to hold to a progressive, causality model. Our continuum is in this linear tradition, yet we know we are all multidimensional. Cross-cultural understanding is helpful in grasping this process for those of us acculturated in the Eurocentric perspective. Opening ourselves to the multiplicity of cultural perspectives in the United States can help us appreciate the breadth of the interdependence of flow and causality, which is unimaginable from a single cultural viewpoint.

For women, movement backward often occurs when we have no energy at the moment to take on yet another man for his dominant ways or when we are in a powerless position, such as with a boss who controls the job we need for economic survival. We give deference, we are manipulative, or perhaps we overcompensate by being helpful. We know what and why we are doing this. It is not the real us, but options are limited. We try to center ourselves in the transition at other times.

Men's backward movement is accomplished by simply standing still. Most of our institutional processes support male-dominant behavior. If we relax our effort to achieve and maintain equity, our well-practiced steps in dominant/subordinant collusion reemerge. There is also the ever-present opportunity to live the benefits of dominance. For example, when another man delineates the importance of career at the expense of family and friends, do I engage in evolutionary dialogue or remain quiet and support the traditional choice of either family or career? Running on automatic maintains the dominator system, so conscious living is required. This is exhausting when we first choose to live differently. After a while we learn to be patient with our relapses.

People of Color and the Continuum

Male/female issues have been opened for discussion in most cultures. In the United States as well as in other Western countries, the effects of white racism have delayed this discussion for many and continue to do so. People of color tend not to do the same level of work on male/female issues that they do on racism. Most men and women of color understandably put racism as an issue ahead of sexism. For instance, the need to bond over blackness may keep many African-American men and women from opening up the subject of dominance and subordinance in their male/female relationships—particularly where black women have considerable authority in their culture.

People of color may find much along this continuum that fits their experience and much that does not. Men of color usually find that in white culture they are considered dominant because of their maleness and subordinant because of their color. Knowing how subordinance feels may give some men insight into women's issues. If a man of color is gay, he has double subordinance. He may have to deal with a definition of maleness that comes from straight, white, male culture—get a job, get a family, and take care of them.

Many women of color find their experience of the woman's journey similar to white women's experience, but with the double subordinant status of being both female and a woman of color. How this status varies within each culture depends on the roles women have been accorded and whether it is politically wise to speak about them. Most women of color who must deal daily with white culture find there is an assumption that they will act like white women are supposed to; therefore, they are treated as if their issues are the same as white women's issues. This assumption makes them as well as their history and their issues invisible. Conversely, when women of color are assertive about their issues, they are sanctioned as uppity and aggressive and find themselves isolated.

Lesbian, Gay, and Bisexual People and the Continuum

Gay, lesbian, and bisexual people's experiences working on gender issues vary widely. Still, we can generalize about some important differences between straight and gay people of which we need to be aware when working with the Male/Female Continuum.

Lesbians may have many of the same issues as straight women, with the added issue of heterosexism—double subordinance. Gay men may have acquired some of the characteristics of dominant straight men, but if they are out as gay or are suspected of being homosexual, they are seen as less than male by homophobic straight men. Focusing on gender issues from only a straight point of view does not, therefore, allow us to ask questions at a level basic enough for lesbians or gay men.

The questions of "Am I male enough?" or "Am I female enough?" are a theme of concern when dealing with the Male/Female Continuum. Straight people do not as often have the depth of anxiety about these questions that gay men and lesbians may have. Our homophobic society makes it difficult for gay- and lesbian-identified people to assume maleness and femaleness as a given.

Straight women are not the only ones who must fight the label of sexual object; both lesbians and gay men must do it as well. Violence based on gender, of which straight women are always aware, is too often focused with added vengeance on both gay men and lesbians. Because of the real possibility of physical violence and ostracism that gay men and lesbians face if their sexuality becomes known, they may have difficulty concentrating on just being male or female on a continuum such as this.

Growing up, if lesbians experienced support for themselves as female, and especially if they had support for their sexual identity, these positive experiences may have produced in them a capacity for independent thought and behavior. They may not have had the typical experience of growing up learning deference and needing male approval. As adults they are likely angry at others' expectations that they should show constant deference, and more aware of the effects of this behavior on all women. However, for a lesbian to assume that a straight woman wants to hear about giving up deference could put a lesbian at risk of exclusion or worse.

Straight-identified bisexual people will likely identify in many ways with straight people's gender issues, because of their identification with straight society. Homosexually identified bisexual people will likely identify with gay and lesbian issues, as well as straight issues, depending on how much experience and time they have spent identifying as straight.

Dealing with Nontransitional People

A woman or man who has moved deep into the transition and lives or works with others who remain in the orange section of role stereotyping encounters many difficulties. We cannot compel others to change. We can change our lives and stop supporting the collusion of dominance and subordinance, though this has its consequences. We never truly know what others have lived through and are currently facing, so it is best to be slow to criticize others for not moving. Even though we accept where others are on their journey, practically we still need to understand the effect of a person in the orange section on someone into the transition and colleagueship.

Women with Men

If as women centered in the transition or colleagueship we are dealing with a man in the orange part of the continuum, we find we may need to adjust our behavior. If we act too differently from what he expects, it may open us to harm. For example, if we are comfortable with power, if we do not depend on traditional courtesies to feel connected or are not continually offering emotional support and help, we will be blamed for the awkwardness of communication. He may avoid us,

41

which is a type of punishment. He can also punish us by calling us aggressive, incompetent, or weak. Our style of handling power may be labeled too overt and pushy or just as readily said to lack firmness. From his point of view in the orange section any behavior outside of what he sees as acceptable for women is wrong. Sharing power and being empowering of others seem indecisive to him.

If we are dealing with a man in the early orange section, we are at risk physically. If he is in the sexual harassment section, he may assume we are open for and even inviting sexual advances, because a woman who is deep into the transition has a sense of excitement and energy around her. Men who still basically respond to women as sex objects see spontaneity and excitement as sexually provocative behaviors. In dominance and subordinance, the freedom to act spontaneously is permitted only when being sexual. Women acting with a sense of energy are sexualized.

It can be problematic for women in transition to live their energy when men who have not come to grips with their sexualizing are present. For example, if a woman in the transition rebuffs the overtures of a man in the orange section who has sexualized her spontaneity, she may find herself accused of turning him on and not playing fair—as if it is her fault that he turned himself on by inappropriately interpreting her energy.

Other than violence, women in the transition find the paternalism of men in the orange section perhaps the hardest behavior with which to deal. The men are so nice. They seem so receptive. However, they are really never reached, even though on the surface they seem quite collegial by always being encouraging. It is almost impossible to talk about how power is managed between us, that is, the way he always seems to have the final say or approval and keeps himself in the position of "letting" us act. How things happen, that is, the process, is never discussed.

The effect is that our anger stays close to the surface, where it is easily tapped. There is no way to deal with its source—his paternalism and need to always be in control. Only by using enormous amounts of energy and time to overcome his resistance to owning his paternalism can we have a chance of reaching him. If we do take him on, there is no guarantee anything will change. His courtesy says he always listens to a lady/woman, but there is no need to act on what is discussed, *especially if retaining dominance is in any way questioned.* The risk in confronting him is that we are accused of being a pushy, angry, woman, while he is such a nice man.

The main way subordinants acting individually can change their status is to talk about the processes in which they find themselves. So, first we have to agree we can talk about our process. Next, the process cannot be talked about until trust is established. We must be able to trust that when perceptions are shared about how relationships or events are perceived, the information gained will not be used against us. Feeling safe is important.

When working with those who are also in the transition, process remarks come quickly and easily. The sad thing is that men in the orange section often misunderstand such remarks as criticism and judgment of them. Therefore, for self-protection with certain men it is sometimes wise to shift quietly back to the courtesy and deference part of the continuum. To not do so with those who are highly regarded by others and/or who carry authority over us may harm us professionally. Whether or not we talk about the consequences of power differentials for us is always a question of time, risk, and how willing the other person is to engage with us.

If we have to step back and stay for long periods in the orange section, the stress can be intense. Once we know how it feels to leave the collusion of role stereotyping, it is difficult to spend much time there again. We pay for it by having our anger constantly on edge. It is important to find partners and friends with whom we can spend substantial amounts of time to give us relief.

Men with Women

As growing numbers of men move into the transition, they find themselves frustrated with women in the orange section. As men, once we make a decision to learn, it becomes increasingly difficult to be around women in the orange section. We are unwilling to accept women's expectations of dependency and manipulation as well as expectations that both of us will continue to play the dominance/subordinance game. The manipulations with which we used to collude and of which we pretended blindness are now irritating.

Women in the orange section remind a man in the transition (blue section) of those things he is angriest about, such as

— his perceived helplessness in relationships with women,

— the emotional costs of always being dominant, and

— manipulative and controlling women who are or have been in his life.

Such women demand our energy so they can be dependent and protected. We have less and less time and energy to respond to such pressure. We are too busy with ourselves and what we have to learn.

Perhaps the hardest situation for heterosexual men occurs when we enter the transition but our partner has not. Her resistance to movement involves her buried anger from our shared history. As a subordinant she learned constantly to bury her anger at her treatment. She felt she was loved because she did this and accepted us as we were.

Perhaps she may have been urging us to look more closely at ourselves, but now that we are willing to do so, there is an implication that she must look at who she is. This may not have been her original expectation. Rather than looking at herself, her anger will likely focus on what we did to her in our dominance, and what we are now failing to do, such as support her financially in her accustomed style. (Many men make job changes in the transition.)

Once a woman agrees to talk about any issue, she is opening the door to admitting that she has been colluding all along with the manipulative ways and power games of a subordinant. When a woman is first to start the movement along the continuum, she more easily owns her part in colluding. The idea can grow on her. It is not thrust upon her as yet another instance when a dominant knows more than she does about how she should be. She is excited because she learned it first and figured it out for herself. This knowledge may be overwhelming, but it is also energizing. She is using her energy to break out of a world where dominants defined her and decided what is important.

There is no way for us as heterosexual men moving into the transition first not to tap unfathomable depths of anger directed at us by our female partners when we first try to open up looking at our process and power differentials. We need support, perhaps a close friend or counselor, to help sort out what our issues are, what her issues are, what we can ask of her, and what as her partner we are helpless to raise. It is not an easy time for either. We need space for rethinking who we are and what we are doing with our life.

We have more options when we are less personally involved with a woman. In fact, in our work life we may find we are in a position to press women to make some changes. If we supervise a traditional woman, we may be able to challenge her with development opportunities. We can urge her to be more direct and responsible for herself. We can define it as part of her job duties that she do some work on personal growth, expand her horizon with course work, and handle a broader range of tasks.

Men in the transition may want to look around and note which women peers they are in the habit of avoiding and which they seek out. Those we are most comfortable with may be those who massage our ego a lot, who play up to us and make us feel masculine. Will we now talk to them about our changes, asking them questions about how they feel? That takes courage. We need to differentiate the women who respond to the new man we feel we are becoming from those who are frightened and probably avoiding us.

Women we paid little attention to in the past may be those who scared or threatened us by being so self-assured that they didn't seem to need us. They didn't allow us to control them. They were unresponsive to such things as the repartee and joking we may have engaged in to feel comfortable—and dominant. We may want to look at these women in new ways—as possible resources for our journey, a part of which is learning to deal with women in the orange section.

Women and Men in Organizations

An organization's products or services influence where men and women in the organization tend to cluster on the continuum. Businesses such as banking and insurance that rely on large numbers of women in low level clerical positions will likely have men clustered in the role-slotting section of the continuum. In religious organizations which depend on women to fill the traditional support role of maintaining the institution, we are likely to find most men in the helpful, paternal part of the orange section because that is what helps keep these women happy and productive.

A business whose industry has a history of few nontraditional jobs for women, such as a foundry or utility company, and has not addressed the issues of changing roles for men and women through internal change projects, will likely find the norm for men (though not for every man individually) to be somewhere between sexual harassment and discrimination. Whether women hold jobs requiring physical strength or not, the product suggests men's work. Women as physical, strong, and independent are far outside men's traditional image. Since the men likely do not differentiate women and still feel protective and physically superior to them, they handle their discomfort by emphasizing men as strong and women as weak, vulnerable, and/or sex objects.

In any work culture, women find it difficult to be very far ahead of where the norm for men is on the continuum. For instance, if the norm for men is in the discrimination section, many women will be grouped in the early transition (and they will be quite angry). If the norm for men is in the paternal area, women find it easier to be in the transition, making the decision that they have much to learn. A gentleman does give a woman some leeway as long as she doesn't require change on his part.

Because over the last thirty-five years our culture has allowed male/female issues to be addressed, most organizations have women who are near the end of the transition and are more than ready to move into colleagueship. There are some men here as well. In organizations where time and effort is spent dealing with these issues, a core of men and women develops that gives stability to the organizational movement along the continuum—though the members may not always be given credit by those in the orange section or they may not perceive themselves as doing so. It is hard for them to see their effect in the aggregate on the organization because they personally receive so many mixed messages and resistance. They are constantly cycled back into their frustration and anger because others misunderstand their intentions and force them to act in ways they no longer wish to act.

One phenomenon beginning to show up in organizations that have worked consistently on these issues for many years is that the norm for men has moved into the early transition. As noted on the continuum, movement into the early transition for both women and men means a surfacing of anger and defensiveness. As a significant number of men enter this early part of the transition, the hostile energy that surfaces can feel threatening.

We are somewhat used to groups of women moving angrily into the transition, but we are not yet used to groups of men doing so. When women enter this phase, others act irritated but usually dismiss them as unimportant. Though this experience is frustrating to women, lack of attention gives women space to do their work in the transition. It is unclear whether men will have such space. Groups of unhappy, complaining men usually get what they say they want, which probably is not what will move them farther into the transition. Rather, their resistance to entering the transition is supported by other men who see no reason to move and by women who "still cater to keeping men happy." One of the steadying things is the many men who have moved well into the transition and give stability to the pressure for needed change in organizations.

Avoiding Competition between Diverse Groups

As organizations address the issues of gender, it is crucial that other issues of discrimination, particularly race, culture, and sexual orientation, be addressed simultaneously. If not, these differences are put in competition with gender and each other. People who represent the diversities not being addressed are put more at risk of intolerant behavior by dominants.

Dominance and subordinance are the basic concern. When being dominant is closed off in only one dimension, a dominant person's need to control others is switched to those whose subordinance is not given attention; *and* subordinants from the group focused on relax their attention to those ways they participate in being the dominant. For instance, if we increase attention to gender discrimination without calling attention to racism, racist behavior or incidents will likely increase in organizational settings. Protection of entitlement, perceived and real, is the basic concern. Given the prevalence of dominance and subordinance, the scramble to be on top in one area moves to another.

When addressing gender concerns, we particularly need to acknowledge the presence of racism and heterosexism. Men and women reflect a wide range of diversity. To see issues only in terms of gender dismisses other diversity that may be represented in the room and puts unacknowledged diversity in competition for recognition.

One reason we find so much cultural resistance to being inclusive is that more and more we are putting together the concerns of all people assigned to subordinance, and there are fewer and fewer groups on which dominants can let loose their need for control. The egalitarianism implied in democracy is not easily achieved. Accepting that we currently live in inequity and continue to live the struggle empowers us and keeps us from the disillusionment of a dream failed.

7 Colleagueship

Feelings of colleagueship with others emerge as we move through the transition into the green part of the continuum. These feelings sometimes lead us to great expectations of ourselves and others, and of the work we do together. Sometimes our expectations are so high they feel judgmental to others—exactly the opposite of what we intend.

Given the enormity of personal and societal resistance to change, it is heartening to find so many groups and organizations committed to exploring and creating equity. Colleagueship and power equity thrive where individuals and groups of people decide to make it happen. The search for gender equity is but part of the larger struggle for recognition, acceptance, and respect for humankind in all its multiplicity.

Our journeys in the transition, which are never finished, increase our understanding of ourselves and the assumptions that have shaped our values and prescribed our behavior. We begin the realignment of our relationships with those of the same and other gender. We open ourselves to diversity and learn about our part in the dynamics of oppression. With others we lay a foundation for power equity and colleagueship. In the transition we reassess our values, changing or reaffirming them within a broader, more life affirming perspective. As women and as men we take time for ourselves in new ways. It is an intensely personal journey. It is an amazingly public journey. We live either/or and both/and mentalities at the same time.

The transition brings insights as to the container of our world-view. We value equality and begin to reach for equity. As we live moments of equity we open ourselves to diversity bringing joy, confusion, passion, fear, and all sorts of new feelings and experiences to our interpersonal and group relationships. We see that the societal transformation, within which our journeys are made possible, is multi-generational. We are frustrated, yet renewed in our struggle, as we see that in our lifetime we will always find parts of ourselves back in the orange section. While it is tempting to equate moving well into and through the transition with having done it all, we cannot assume that what we learned in the transition is all we need to know.

If we moved out ahead of our friends, partners, and work associates to do the work of the transition we appreciate those who have grown with us. We grieve the lost connections with those who do not struggle with us or were unwilling to give room in their relationship with us for us to do what we are about. We are determined never again to let another person's journey take precedence over our own. We are determined to never assume that our life has precedence over someone else's. Yet we expect that in colleagueship, the experience of power equity should include feelings of caring, respect, acceptance, and connection—and rightly so. The ups and downs of life are real to us as we live them. Without the prescription of normal as a constant positive, we experience our gyrations without negative self-judgment.

In the transition, as women and men we traveled parallel journeys. These journeys have been slowly intertwining with those of the other gender. How we perceive ourselves, our family, our friends, lovers, work, and the world has slowly changed. It is hard to remember the person we once were. Possibilities and expectations for working in relationships and groups have grown. As we became less defensive, our personal resistance to doing the work necessary to create and sustain colleagueship was lowered. The basic resistance is always to looking fully at the process in which we live with others.

We remember when we thought colleagueship was present when we had a mutually accepted experience of being ladies and gentlemen (subordinance and dominance, with no questions raised). The best we could do was "you go first for awhile and, then, I will." Whereas these behaviors are options, they are not what we mean now when we use the terms *colleagueship* and *partnership*.

Building a Mosaic of Friendships

Colleagueship brings a mosaic of friendships. In the gentleman-and-lady part of the orange section, our primary relationships supposedly sit on top of a hierarchy of other relationships, although a man's relationships take precedence over a woman's. Such a hierarchy implies that all relationships are heterosexual. Figure 1 shows the priority of these relationships. In colleagueship, if and when we choose a primary relationship, we perceive this as the center of a mosaic of relationships, with each one having its own integrity. No one relationship fills all our needs, though a primary one fills many. This mosaic feels different from a pyramid of relationships. Commitment to another person centers our life and gives us stabili-

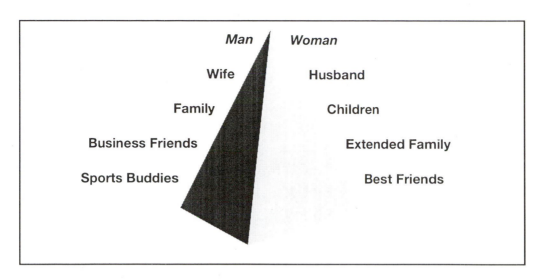

Figure 1. *A pyramid of relationships.*

ty, the basis for family development, and space for personal growth and intimacy. Commitment is done thoughtfully and consciously, understanding the importance of building the foundation for a relationship and the lifelong work it takes to create and maintain healthy connections. See the mosaic of relationships in figure 2. All relationships are thought of in terms of commitment, though some are not as deep as others. None are entered into lightly because each takes time and care. The more central the relationship is in our life, the more time and care it needs. Our partners, friends, family, and work colleagues all have a place in our mosaic. Each relationship is considered important enough to keep in repair.

People come in and out of such a friend system, giving it a feeling of fluidity; some stay a long time and others a short while. Because each person is centered in her or his own journey, the mosaic itself is mobile. If a person is away for awhile, he or she usually enters the system quickly again when paths cross, taking up where each left off. It takes work and time to stay connected, so a connection varies with how much time each person has to put into it at any given moment. Looking back, we may note that as we moved along our journeys, many friendships dropped away and new ones emerged.

Colleagueship opens up the creative possibilities in each of us. We bring to it our full energy and creative self, giving the interpersonal connection an intensity that is unexpected at first. Our full energy includes our sexual self. Discussing how and when to set boundaries becomes important. One of the tension points of moving into and through the transition is that those close to us, who have not moved into the transition, feel the impact of the closeness of many of our friendships. This can raise fears in our partner that a shared relationship is disintegrating. We remember well how easily in the orange section cross-gender relationships for

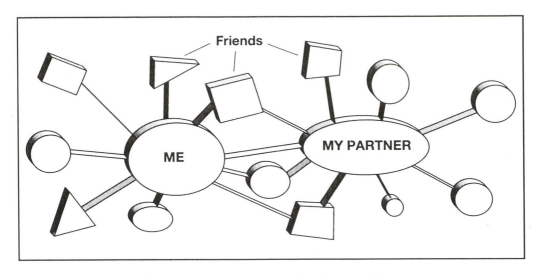

Figure 2. *A mosaic of relationships.*

straight people were suspected of being sexual even when they were not, so that many friendships were lost. We (straight folk) get a taste now of what it is like for gay men, lesbians, and bisexual people when straight people assume all their same-sex relationships are sexual.

In the transition the term *relationship* took on a meaning broader than implying sexual intimacy. A wide range of friendship possibilities opened up. Intimacy and closeness are now differentiated from needing to be sexual. Although they may be combined, it is understood that they need not be. A partner still in the orange section has little information that says close relationships between straight men and women can be anything but sexual. In the blue section, friendships grew to include a variety of people. Gender, sexual orientation, race, age, class, and physical abilities are not limiting factors.

Comfort with personal growth, an understanding of relationship, an ability to work in process, a facility to say what is true for ourselves, a capacity to stay with issues that push our personal boundaries, an ability to be in present time, and the insight to know that no one can have it all together all the time underline the fluidity needed to function in a mosaic of relationships. Much of what we learned as we journeyed through the transition gives us the skills needed for the give and take of personal relationships, other friendships, and collegial work relationships. A new sense of humor which was created with others and is pointed at ourselves probably emerged in the transition. It helps sustain us on our journeys together. We are not just comfortable with diverse people in our support systems and networks but seek such differences as gender, race, culture, sexual orientation, age, differently abled, and class. It feels uncomfortable not to have such diversity of people as friends and colleagues.

As we approach the colleagueship section, less attention is given to distinguishing between women's and men's journeys. There is more commonality in the elements, although diversity is present in how they are expressed by each.

Some Important Elements of Colleagueship

The elements of colleagueship displayed in the green section of the continuum have no particular developmental order. Most are intertwined and complementary to each other. Colleagueship remains a developmental and creative process. These elements are looked at through the changes we made as we moved from the orange section through the blue section into the green.

At first, in the orange section, role stereotyping ascribed one set of characteristics to femaleness and another to maleness. These characteristics often had little to do with our actual personal characteristics as individual men and women. In the transition we did the painful work of looking inside for lost parts of ourselves. This process will probably never end. In colleagueship, however, the emphasis is on exploring balance and wholeness within each of us. The images of men as self-sufficient and women as dependent are gone. Healthy interdependence and caring for others are what is important. Both women and men raise process issues and keep us focused on tasks. How tasks are accomplished is as important as doing the task. **The process and task are both acknowledged and considered integral** in everything we do.

In equitable relationships the process of how things happen is as important as what is done, talked about, or accomplished. What we do and think are never so important that they overshadow how something is done. In fact, paying attention to the process first, making sure it is inclusive and values diversity, shortens the time for doing the work, making everyone more creative in the process.

In white culture we assume a task will connect us and relationships will develop out of the work we do together. This assumption probably comes from a combination of our rational, causality way of thinking and our work ethic. White culture is the only culture that typically works this way. Cultures of color put the relationship first. No task can be undertaken until a relationship has been established. Individuals in their diversity are acknowledged in this way. Caring and trust are built, and the task when addressed is often accomplished in significantly less time. To be inclusive of people of color means paying attention to relationships and valuing connection both interpersonally and within a group.

When starting tasks and projects with a new group of people, we facilitate the tasks by taking time to get to know each other and the resources each brings. We also need to give time to discussing how we will work together. At meetings, regular, brief check-ins to find out how each member is doing and what is happening in his or her life continue the spirit of colleagueship. How personal or business-focused these check-ins are depends on the members' expectations, trust that has been built between them, and the time available. Regularly giving time to discuss how group members are working together—that is, naming the process they are embedded in—is critical.

The etiquette and skill of naming the process we share in relationships and groups ask that sometimes we balance this naming with simply living the process awhile. "Talking process" can become so enticing—or boring—that we get caught up in endless discussion. Sometimes we need to let go of sharing our view of how we perceive the dynamics around us and just live it. After hearing each other's ideas and concerns, we may agree to specific action or we just let what we have heard affect what we do—not talking issues to death but each adjusting how he or she behaves. We need the space to live the process awhile and not put every detail into words. **Naming the process** needs to **balance living the process,** that is, letting things happen now that we know how each feels and thinks.

In colleagueship both partners **share responsibility for** taking care of their **relationship.** In the orange section, the woman did this work as best she could, raising concerns about how it was going or how it felt. We have grown in sharing the responsibility for relationships for some time now. The transition time ripped loose the relationship from the way each person tried to control it from his or her one-up or one-down position. In the green section, concern about the relationship and appreciation for it come from both partners.

The power equity of colleagueship demands a **contextual view** of seeing ourselves as part of a whole as well as individualized. **Linear thinking,** which predominates in Western, white cultural thought patterns, gets in the way of perceiving process contextually. Linear thinking leads to seeing the world only through a problem-solving mode: if A is taken care of, then we can move on to B, and so forth. A contextual view assumes that a segment of experience represents the whole, as in a hologram. It also means surrounding a problem or task with constant data collection, keeping many avenues of solutions open simultaneously. A wholeness pervades the process rather than the single-mindedness of one path, decided on early in a decision-making process and held to rigidly.

Joan Schriber Smith further delineates contextual thinking, as described here, into circular and organic experiences of life.[1] She says that for a linear-oriented person, the answer to the question "Why are we here?" is to progress; for a circular-oriented person the answer is to connect; and for an organic-oriented person it is to love. If each were to answer the question "What is real?" the linear-oriented person would say "that which is fact," the circular-oriented person would say personal experience, and the organic-oriented person would say knowing or intuition. Different cultures, as well as men and women within cultures, differ in their focus on such qualities. *Contextual frame of reference,* as used here, includes the circular and organic modes of life, and supports keeping our options open as long as possible because of the active flow of data throughout the process.

Old habits of being exclusively linear in our thinking prevent us from being aware of the processes we are in. To become aware requires not only seeing how everyone else fits in, but including ourselves in the context. In the orange section, dominants see others doing things without taking into account their own presence and effect on others, one of which is how they assume control of people and events. In the blue section, the fast pace of new awareness makes us feel as if we are the center of events, overly responsible for everything that happens around us. Men become aware of how central they keep themselves. They often keep their centrality just by the intense work they do in struggling to change. (What a no-win situation!) Both men and women often overreact in the transition by being overwhelmed with their new awareness of themselves and their effect on others. The green section of colleagueship asks that we act and see ourselves in context but not as central. We affect everything and everything affects us, but no more than anyone else. As everyone shares their perceptions of the process we are in, a picture closer to the whole emerges based on the diversity of the people present.

The equity of colleagueship asks us to withhold judgment while continually taking in information. The flow of data is vital because in colleagueship almost everything that happens needs to be open for the possibility of discussion. In role stereotyping we learn immediately to put all we hear into value judgments—good or bad, right or wrong. In relationships where equity is valued, we move away from either/or thinking. We assume everyone is doing the best they can and trust that they know themselves well enough to share what is happening for them and what they need. We also accept that others can give us information and insight about ourselves and interactions which expand our awareness.

Being nonjudgmental starts with valuing the justice and fairness implied in democracy and in the U.S. with first amendment rights to freedom of speech. We agree to disagree. We can trust others in colleagueship and equity when we share a value system based on respect for diversity and mutual empowerment. Valuing diversity means that disagreements become the sharing of information about our diversity rather than arguments for rightness. If, when dealing with those in the orange section, we find our basic rights of justice and fairness are being compromised, we must consider if our safety is in jeopardy and, then, reasons for staying in dialogue. The outcomes of these considerations determine whether we stay or leave.

Being nonjudgmental is not a singular act. It is a stance taken in a context with others. It is helpful to talk about the difference between naming and labeling, so that agreement on how things are heard is clear. Each person agrees that stating what she or he perceives will be heard as naming, not as labeling or being judgmental. Important work for both women and men in the transition was to become less defensive in how they heard what others said. Now more data are received as others describing what is true for them (naming), and less as reflective of personal judgment on the receiver (labeling). Our trust of others grows as we perceive them in the context of their life experience.

The integrity of how we respond supports our being perceived as nonjudgmental. If subsequently we are genuinely inclusive, supportive, and caring toward those whose behavior we have described and we do not demand that our observations are "right," we will be perceived as nonjudgmental. If we are noninclusive, nonsupportive, and noncaring, with an air of superiority, then we will be heard as labeling others.

Much judging comes from observing and feeling strong emotional reactions in others, without sharing impressions of what we saw and felt or allowing for our own projections. The experience of such reactions is left unfinished if we do not share our impressions in hindsight. We have been learning to do this. We sometimes feel uncomfortable asking what others felt, as if we are invading their space, or perhaps we are afraid of what we will hear. In colleagueship we respect the right of others to say no when we ask them about their feelings, but we share the belief that it is all right to ask.

If we do not or cannot ask about someone's reaction, then we need to act on the assumption that we do not know the meaning of the emotions they express. We need to be aware of when we are making judgments and projections as if we knew. It is hard to avoid this behavior when we have felt strong emotional reactions to us or others but have no substantiation of their meaning.

Sharing how things are going needs to include talking about how we may still collude to hold each other in role stereotyping. It will be awhile before we have more support to be outside role stereotyping than to conform to it, because of the culture we are embedded in. We have habits and ways of thinking that we grew up with which, for a long time, automatically put us back in dominance and subordinance. It's not "bad" that we slip back, but when living and/or working closely with others in equitable relationships, regularly **talking about how each still colludes to keep a relationship inequitable** is important. This conversation requires a give and take in **sharing feedback.**

Feedback, to be useful, needs to be considered a gift, not criticism. When giving it, we are describing, not analyzing or judging. When receiving it, we are collecting data. No one person knows all each one of us needs to know about ourselves. Feedback from one person must be added to what others say and then thoughtfully allowed to affect us. This is one reason why a mosaic of friendships is so important.

Not all feedback is verbal. Much is given in the form of body language and emotional expression. Our intuitive feelings about another say a great deal. Much of what we intuit is based on the emotional impact of another person. **Emotional input is therefore appreciated** as well as **intellectual input.** The impact of colleagueship, where we strive to share power, engages our emotions more frequently and for longer periods than we could ever have foreseen. This in itself feels different.

The violent end of the orange section brought terror for women and self-destructive feelings of superiority for men. In the late part of the orange section—the gentleman-and-lady syndrome of buried feelings of anger—negative emotions were never expressed. Emotions were to be kept under control between men and women, with as little fluctuation as possible, except for some times of pleasure. Spontaneity was out of place.

In the transition, our emotions seemed to go wild with sharp peaks and valleys as we stumbled and searched for who we are and would like to be. As we entered the transition, our emotions of pain and anger were overwhelming—for women, anger at enduring subordinance; for men, anger at their co-optation into the confinement of dominance; for both, anger at each other for perceived hurts for unmet expectations. Once both men and women made the decision to learn about their own dominance and subordinance, their emotional swings were sharp and wide. Emotional highs reflected the discovery of new insights and the excitement that comes from learning. There was also the pain of facing the truth about our behavior, the aloneness of being responsible for ourselves, the realization of the pain caused to others, and the difficulty of changing life-long habits. Figure 3 diagrams the changes in our emotions as we moved from role stereotyping into the transition.

The question becomes What will our emotional life be like in power equity? Will it be kept within a narrow spectrum as in the lady-and-gentleman part of the orange section, or move sharply as in the transition? Actually, we have little choice. Once we value sharing our feelings and talking about the processes we are in, our emotions are constantly engaged. Learning to live with our emotions in real time is part of equity. Figure 4 shows the progression of figure 3 through colleagueship, where we continue to experience a full range of emotions as the norm.

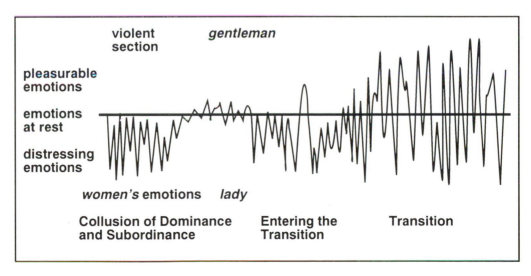

Figure 3. *Experiencing the change in our emotions when moving into the transition.*

55

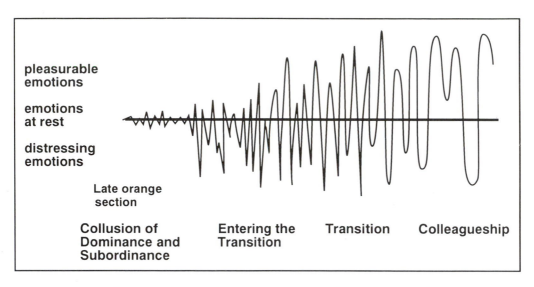

Figure 4. *The intensity of emotions along the continuum.*

This full range of emotions is not what we expected colleagueship to be like. Equity means getting used to wide swings in our emotional life as normal. If we are white and/or straight, we have come to grips with our need for centrality, that is, expecting others to adjust to us, or acting white and/or straight. As multiplicity and diverse ways are expressed more, our emotions are engaged in more ways. As we move outside of dominance and subordinance, the engaging of our emotions in such ways is less painful and more satisfying. Our emotional life brings a sense of aliveness. Much of white, middle-class culture has always been characterized by tighter, more controlled emotions than many other cultures.

With our emotions so active, it is important that our feelings be connected to our intellect. **Connecting our feelings and intellect** is the product of listening to how another feels and thinks, and then letting it affect how we think, feel, and act. How we respond, what we say, what we decide to do are all affected by what we have heard and observed. Our behavior changes because we care about how others feel and what they say.

Equity asks that we differentiate ourselves, that we act autonomously within context. The ability to do this is an important outcome of moving through the transition, especially for those women moving away from deference and helplessness. For those who are a part of white, middle-class culture, subordinance allowed a woman to have the illusion of living in constant attachment. Dependency fosters this. The transition forces these women to become more differentiated and learn to move to inclusiveness as a choice. Living in a constant state of attachment makes others feel us as clinging and possessive. We are unable to be centered in our journey. In the transition we learn how difficult it is to get angry at someone with whom we are in constant attachment, because if we do we are really angry at ourselves. This causes much self-blame. For the other person to be angry at us is almost unbearable. For those women whose life experience has encouraged or demanded being differentiated, developing more permeable boundaries to be inclusive and vulnerable is asked for, which is similar to what is being asked of many men.

In the orange section, men are expected to be autonomous, independent, and self-contained. When autonomy and dominance are glued together, it means that a relationship with another is synonymous with the dominant, not inclusive of both people in the relationship. As a dominant man moves through the transition, learning that a relationship is separate from him, he may feel as though a jacket he thought was part of his skin is being forcibly removed. We carry the pain of the removal with the joy of being able to see the relationship as we go forward. The task of shedding the jacket of dominance in the transition can be such hard work that we may believe that is all that needs to be done. But it is not enough to peel off this jacket and separate dominance from autonomy, without also making our boundaries permeable. For men to live in equity then means they perceive a relationship as different from themselves and attend to it consciously by willingly talking about it (processing), and they loosen personal boundaries in order to be inclusive, connected, and vulnerable. For both men and women, equity requires that we value being able to shift between **autonomy** and the **inclusiveness** of feeling **connected.**

The basic principle of equity—to regularly name the process—keeps **flexibility and options** alive. The roles each assumes can expand as possibilities are named and explored. Colleagueship presumes that each is willing to try different ways to do things as well as give others a chance to do what we have usually done. How leadership is shared is a major function of keeping options open. In equitable relationships and groups, our time for a leadership role will come. We need to follow our intuition when suddenly we feel it is our turn to assume leadership, and, just as quickly, we must be ready when we sense leadership needs to pass on to someone else.

The word *colleagueship* has obviously taken on special meanings and feelings. It certainly refers to more than two people who just happen to work together. The dynamics and principles of equity are brought into the core meaning of colleagueship. Both personal and work relationships are included.

Some results of colleagueship can be predicted:

— Diversity will be expressed and valued.

— We will feel mutually empowered.

— The creative expression in each will be enhanced.

— There will be a feeling of *new dynamics* around us, a sense of constantly renewing energy.

The power equity of colleagueship is never set or finished. Taking our relationships with others seriously requires us to take care of ourselves physically, mentally, psychically, and spiritually. The closer we live and work with others, the more painful and disorienting approaching burnout is to ourselves and others. Making space for ourselves, our work, our partners, our friends, and work colleagues becomes a balancing act. Moving along our journey intensifies the need to be clear and realistic about what we want to do and whom we want to be. Finding intimacy and support are healthy responses. We need to take care of ourselves. Renewal is a constant challenge as we work to make this world a better place in which to live.

8 Looking Ahead on our Journeys

In closing, we ask the question Where are we now as a culture? Two things important in moving us on our journeys are our commitments as individuals to movement and the support we receive in a democracy from the legal system. These two are intertwined. That the legal system lags behind what is desired and acceptable to a majority of citizens is frustrating to those of us working for gender equity. Legal scholar Catharine MacKinnon says, "Equality will require change, not reflection—a new jurisprudence, a new relation between life and law. Law that does not dominate life is as difficult to envision as a society in which men do not dominate women. . . . the legitimacy of existing law is based on force at women's expense. Women have never consented to its rule—suggesting that the system's legitimacy needs repair that women are in a position to provide."[1]

Sexism, as racism and heterosexism, is an integral part of the United States legal system. Using it to bring about or consolidate gender equality will be at best a long and arduous process. The treatment of women described in the early orange part of this continuum has been prohibited by law for a long time. Nevertheless, many women are still murdered, mutilated, battered, and raped on the street and in homes every day. Women are still coerced, intimidated, touched, teased, and excluded in institutions whose policies and rules go beyond legal requirements.

The law does not make it inherently safe for women, and the legal process often reflects historical bias in favor of men's right to do what they want to women. There have been important changes in the law, but, the law and the legal process still lag far behind the values held by the majority of citizens (most women and many men). As our society slowly moves into what we describe as the first stages of the transition, physical violence and verbal abuse seem to increase. We appreciate the support the legal system can give through affirmative action and sexual harassment laws. But there are limits to what laws can accomplish and limits to what a legal system with an ingrained bias of men over women will permit.

We support those women and men who seek to relegitimize our legal system to give equal voice to women and men. We see legal systems as reflective of the culture and therefore of only limited usefulness in bringing about the fundamental changes needed for our society to reflect gender equality and equity. For us, equality can be advocated and supported through law and policy. *Equality* supports treating individual people in the same way. Equality says men and women have the same right to such things as job opportunities, physical safety, credit, and health and insurance benefits. *Equity* assumes equality and goes further. Equity recognizes the group and individual particularities of each person and weighs them in an interaction that facilitates potential realization without oppression. Equity is a vision realized in the struggle to live it.

When you are a woman in the early orange section, struggling to survive each day, you want to be treated equally with men as a human being. Having support in the law is necessary yet not sufficient in the end to accomplish what you need. That traditional men have defined themselves as human to the exclusion of women is something to be addressed by those women and men farther along the continuum.

We have many voices as women and men. We speak from our experience with varying wants, needs, and goals. We wish the law could protect and force everyone to move, yet as our awareness increases we realize more clearly that the needed changes are deeper and more pervasive than the law. We use the law to its limits where possible, but it is the commitment of sufficient numbers of women and men that will establish gender equality and create gender equity.

We know what typical male and female journeys to colleagueship are like. We are aware of the significant effect on our culture when large numbers of women enter the transition, as has happened since the late 1960s and 1970s. Everyone is touched. Many men have also entered the transition, enough to effect the norms of many organizations.

The entry of women into the transition was marked in the 1970s by the anger of subordinants who were organizing and making their voices heard in the media. The phenomenon of women's anger piercing through the narrow, prescribed boundaries of tradition has been an ongoing reality.

As growing numbers of men move into the transition, their experience as dominants is no smoother that women's. Early in the transition, men, one by one and occasionally in small groups, struggle to understand what a woman or women want and then find that their own work is about self-discovery and personal growth, a journey that goes far beyond adjusting to what women want.

This personal development attracts little media attention. What does get attention are the political tactics of two quite differing groups of men. Gay and bisexual men (along with lesbians) use demonstrations and other public attention-getting techniques to do the important work of fighting heterosexism and homophobia.

Another group of men who organize in public forums are those who resist the trend of equity between men and women. Such men react defensively to the women and men who are working for more egalitarian gender relations. Men in these reactive groups can be quite offensive when they attack those who advocate equity. They defend traditional family values, men's responsibilities to women and women's duty to men, "God's way," and all things that promote an order where men are dominant. A favorite tactic is to get media coverage of women who accept male dominance.

Such groups do their best to stimulate gender, race, sexual orientation, and cultural bias, fear, and hatred. The upsurge in fundamentalism, the popularity of reactionary talk shows, and the activities of the many organizations that oppose women who choose to control their own lives and bodies are for the most part led by men reacting to the movement of large numbers of women into the transition. Reactionary men reserve a special vindictiveness for men who are in transition. They take every opportunity to sanction and belittle them. This reaction led by the more conservative or fringe groups and spokespeople is supported by men who wish to keep the entitlement they live as a birthright. The increased active resistance in society is an indicator of the pervasiveness of change. Substantial numbers of men are moving into the transition. Their defiance and disregard of the old order along with the much-longer-term actions of feminists (and those women who reject the word *feminist* but live the reality) are bringing about a more intense resistance by those reactionaries who want to maintain it. In the United States we have moved beyond the innovators and early adapters to change, to feeling the impact of the large middle group of people who, as long as they remain oblivious, perpetuate the old order. That many in this group are listening and making changes themselves give those of us who work for gender equity renewed energy. More important, the increased numbers of women and men in transition mean increased momentum on this cultural journey.

Men as a group have yet to get a sense of what the collection of individual journeys means to them. Many men are acquiring skills and developing abilities that facilitate connecting with others. They are learning to be responsible for their own spiritual life and physical well-being. They are attending to their own emotional well-being and are learning not to need always to be center stage. The syntheses of our learning has not yet jelled in enough men to impact society and move men as a group to join in the creation of gender equity for society as a whole.

It is important to remember here the result of men acting as if their journeys are similar to women's. This notion gives men permission to push further into being autonomous, differentiated, and unconnected. For instance, a substantial group of straight and gay men enjoy a lifestyle of wealth and independence promoted as the good life. They feel liberated and often think of themselves as supporting women's liberation. It is a tempting way to live! They have adopted the transition goals for a woman's journey—autonomy and self-reliance. On the surface they appear to be urbane and to have it all. The middle-age crises of large numbers of men who think they escaped the order of the pre-1960s, yet feel an intense aloneness and lack of intimacy and connection, may be what moves us more substantially into the transition. The goal of feeling connected without being possessive, and inclusive without owning another or others, is in the consciousness of many men.

The desire for intimacy and feeling more connected is what propels men into the transition. Separating masculinity from dominance *and* gaining a sense of energy based on one's own unique sense of power move us on through the transition. Dominance through technology and technical solutions is the present way of power in the world. This limited sense of power, which fosters win/lose competition, is literally destroying us. Power remains a "pie" to be cut up, not something to share which grows and expands as we empower others.

Since a man's journey in the transition is more internal and personal than the outer-directed journey of a woman, it feels different as large numbers of men move into the transition beyond the point of **making a decision to learn.** We may hear little at the cultural level, except as individual stories are told. It is not a mass political movement, though many men meet regularly in men's groups for support for individual and systemic change.

We've given much attention to men in this closing section because for us a crucial question is How will we support and encourage men to move into the transition? The question is not *whether* substantial numbers of men will enter it, but how and when.

For women and men the goal is the same—becoming balanced human beings each responsible for their own development as connective, loving, and caring people, *and* independent and differentiated, living in context with each other. How we get there depends on where we start. If we were raised blocking our connective tendencies, our task is different than if we grew up specializing in them. The small steady steps needed to make the journey can seem as if there is no movement at all, and regressions make it hard to see progress. We authors see progress and are hopeful, though realistic about the work ahead of us.

Life is not simple. If it were we could concentrate on the issues of gender in an exclusive manner. In fact, many of us who have tried to do so only find that if we are white and straight, these are what get responded to. For instance, it is white, straight, middle-class women who set the agenda for gender work in the United States, which creates blind spots in the gender journeys for both white women and men.Only women and men oblivious to the dominance of whiteness and straightness in the United States attempt to move through the transition period described in this continuum without reference to race, culture, sexual orientation, and other diversities used by our dominator system to sustain itself. This is not a condemnation of individuals opening to their oppressive domination but rather a call for all, and here, particularly, those straight white women and men on a gender journey, to raise their awareness of the interrelation of various forms of oppression at the societal, group, and individual level.

The agenda for gender work must always be inclusive. Gender equity is not about giving straight white women and men or straight men of color the opportunity to oppress. An African-American woman colleague who works extensively with U.S. corporations notes greater distance and avoidance of her by white women as they make it. A white woman colleague notes a tendency of some men of color to bond with white men in dismissing her's and other women's contributions. A tendency in the dominator system is to use subordinants to do the dirty work of controlling others and maintaining order. This system is used as effectively today as it was when slaves were used as overseers to control other slaves or as when early in this century finishing schools used women to train younger women in the fine art of serving men.

We must learn when we trade on dominance and when on subordinance. We must also learn that the exclusive focus on gender is part of a continuing process in which white, straight women and men keep themselves central—a centrality that perpetuates their dominance. The interplay of gender, race, sexual orientation, and class is a reality of our society. Accepting that it is and avoiding the luxury of confusion and depressive overload that are the exclusive province of dominants are necessary if we are to move on the struggle toward equity.

By putting together the continuum on Sexual Orientation and Identity and the Black/White Continuum in White Culture with the Male/Female Continuum,[2] readers can gain insights into the interconnection of these issues. For instance, a white straight woman can note that on the Male/Female Continuum in the late orange section, maternalism is described as a way to control that sphere of life where we are allowed power—the family and social arena. This is a way to survive the numbing courtesy of paternalistic dismissal behavior. However, on the Black/White Continuum, maternalism is on the dominant white journey along with paternalism. Maternalism can be used to stay dominant where race and culture are concerned. White men sense that white women can be as dominant in their white maternalism as men are in their white paternalism. A white woman will not give up the benefits of her maternalism as a subordinant until she deals with her maternalism as a dominant.

In the transition of the Male/Female Continuum, a straight white woman's lack of inclusiveness of lesbian and bisexual women and their communities reflects her oblivious heterosexism on the dominant's journey along the Sexual Orientation continuum. She may be nervous around lesbians in both white and lesbians-of-color communities, not having dealt with her strong feelings about homosexuality, her terror of speaking on issues of homosexuality, or her fear of color which is mixed up with her homophobia. Her issues of role slotting and discounting are as alive as those of a man in the orange section of the Male/Female Continuum.

Control is always an issue when dealing with change. Our journeys are never completed by looking at how we stay in control of others on just one dimension. A white man who is seriously moving along the men's journey cannot finish his work on staying in control of women until he understands his journey as a white person on this issue. Otherwise, he assumes men of color have the same control issues he does. Men of color are more likely focused on the limits set on their maleness by white racism. Straight men, oblivious to heterosexism, act as if gay and bisexual men are not real men. For most men, intense and often violent childhood experiences that enforce a prohibition of homosexuality must be dealt with in order for men to explore maleness outside of dominance. Gender, race, sexual orientation, and class are all parts of the exploration.

Though women of many cultures share a feeling for being contextual in their outlook on life, the rationality of white culture invades white women's perspectives. This quality will probably remain hidden until white women see themselves on a journey of understanding the culture of whiteness and its effects on "knowing" and the ways rationalistic thought patterns are supported.

Straight men's and women's work in the transition of connecting with other men and women is inhibited by homophobic fears. Until straight people let go of their fears of gay men, lesbians, and bisexual people, and of themselves being perceived as gay or lesbian, their work on the Male/Female Continuum cannot move through the transition.

The excitement of our journeys helps push us through our fears of the complexities of this work. As we become aware of the diversities we represent, the appreciation for differences grows, forming the basis for who we are.

We hope that by describing more clearly the paths we are on as women and men, and catching a glimpse of how gender issues intertwine with those of other human diversities, the journey on the Male/Female Continuum will be enriched. Those who have moved along their journeys need to be perceived as representing the normal, natural way to be; they need to receive recognition for their work and support for being the role models we need.

We travel together!

Bon voyage!

N O T E S

Chapter 1

1. Quoted by Prof. Magoroh Maruyama, Southern Illinois University, in "The Magic of Magoroh Maruyama," *The Tarrytown Letter* (Tarrytown House Executive Conference Center, Tarrytown, NY, November 1992.) Newsletter no longer published.

2. Heather Wishik and Carol Pierce, *Sexual Orientation and Identity: Heterosexual, Lesbian, Gay, and Bisexual Journeys* (Laconia, NH: New Dynamics Publications, 1995).

3. Linda Thomas, Carol Pierce, Rick Huntley, Sharon Bueno Washington, David Wagner, & Lennox Joseph, *Journeys of Race and Culture: Paths to Valuing Diversity* (Laconia, NH: New Dynamics Publications, 1999). This continuum, which is the basis for a forthcoming book, is currently in graphic form only.

Chapter 2

1. *The Report of the Commission on Obscenity and Pornography* (Washington, DC: U.S. Government Printing Office, 1970). Majority report.

2. Terrence Crowley, "The Lie of Entitlement," in *Transforming a Rape Culture*, ed. Emilie Buchwald, Pamila Fletcher, and Martha Roth (Minneapolis, MN: Milkweed Editions, 1993), 374.

Chapter 3

1. The material on survival behavior is taken from Carol Pierce, *Beyond Victim Behavior: Women and Their Socialization* (formerly *Women and Victim Behavior*) (Laconia, NH: New Dynamics Publications, 1984, 1991, 2004).

Chapter 5

1. Wishik and Pierce, "Questioning Assumptions, Expanding Ourselves and Relationships: Transitions for Heterosexual and Heterosexually Identified Bisexual People," Chapter 7, in *Sexual Orientation and Identity*.

Chapter 7

1. Joan Schriber Smith, "The Line, the Circle, and the Globe: Reflections on Reality," manuscript, 1990.

Chapter 8

1. Catharine A. MacKinnon, *Toward a Feminist Theory of the State* (Cambridge: Harvard University Press, 1989), 249.

2. Wishik and Pierce, *Sexual Orientation and Identity*; Thomas and Pierce, *A Black/White Continuum*.

SUGGESTED READING

Dominance and Subordinance

Brownmiller, Susan. *Against Our Will: Men, Women, and Rape*. New York: Bantam, 1975.

Eskenazi, Marin, and David Gallin, eds. *Sexual Harassment: Know Your Rights*. New York: Carroll and Graf, 1992.

Faludi, Susan. *Backlash: The Undeclared War against American Women*. New York: Crown, 1991.

French, Marilyn. *The War against Women*. New York: Summit Books, 1992.

Friday, Nancy. *My Mother, Myself*. New York: Dell, 1987.

Jones, Ann. *Next Time, She'll Be Dead: Battering and How to Stop It*. Boston: Beacon Press, 1994.

Miller, Jean Baker. *Toward a New Psychology of Women*. Boston: Beacon Press, 1986.

Pierce, Carol. *Beyond Victim Behavior: Women and Their Socialization* (formerly *Women and Victim Behavior*). Laconia, NH: New Dynamics Publications, 1984, 1991. Monograph.

Webb, Susan L. Step Forward: *Sexual Harassment in the Workplace, What You Need to Know*. New York: MasterMedia, 1991.

Wolf, Naomi. *The Beauty Myth*. New York: William Morrow, 1991.

The Transition

Anzaldua, Gloria, ed. *Making Face, Making Soul, Haciendo Caras: Creative and Critical Perspectives by Women of Color*. San Francisco: aunt lute foundation, 1990.

Asian Women United of California, ed. *Making Waves: An Anthology of Writings by and about Asian American Women*. Boston: Beacon Press, 1989.

Baraff, Alvin. *Men Talk: How Men Really Feel about Women, Sex, Relationships, and Themselves*. New York: Dutton, 1991.

Bridges, William. *Transitions: Making Sense of Life's Changes*. Reading, MA: Addison-Wesley, 1980.

Buchwald, Emilie, Pamela Fletcher, and Martha Roth, eds. *Transforming a Rape Culture*. Minneapolis: Milkweed Editions, 1993.

Christ, Carol P. *Diving Deep and Surfacing: Women Writers on Spiritual Quest.* Boston: Beacon Press, 1986.

Collins, Patricia Hill. *Black Feminist Thought: Knowledge, Consciousness, and the Politics of Empowerment.* New York: Routledge, 1990.

Eisler, Riane. *The Chalice and the Blade: Our History, Our Future.* San Francisco: Harper and Row, 1988.

Giddings, Paula. *When and Where I Enter: The Impact of Black Women on Race and Sex in America.* New York: Bantam Books, 1988.

Hopcke, Robert H. *Men's Dreams, Men's Healing.* Boston: Chambhala, 1990.

Hull, Gloria T., Patricia Bell Scott, and Barbara Smith, eds. *All the Women Are White, All the Blacks Are Men, But Some of Us Are Brave.* Old Westbury, NY: Feminist Press, 1982.

Hutchins, Loraine, and Lani Kaahumanu, eds. *Bi Any Other Name: Bisexual People Speak Out.* Boston: Alyson Publications, 1991.

Josefowitz, Natasha. *Paths to Power: A Woman's Guide from First Job to Top Executive.* Reading, MA: Addison-Wesley, 1990.

Keen, Sam. *Fire in the Belly: On Being a Man.* New York: Bantam Books, 1992.

Kundtz, David. *Men and Feelings: Understanding the Male Experience.* Deerfield Beach, FL: Health Communications, Inc., 1991.

Maclean, Norman. *A River Runs Through It and Other Stories.* New York: Pocket Books, 1992. Fiction.

Montuori, Alfonso, and Isabella Conti. *From Power to Partnership.* San Francisco: Harper and Row, 1993.

Osherson, Samuel. *Finding Our Fathers: How a Man's Life Is Shaped by His Relationship with His Father.* New York: Fawcett Columbine, 1987.

Pharr, Suzanne. *Homophobia: A Weapon of Sexism.* Inverness, CA: Chardon Press, 1988.

Phelps, Stanlee, and Nancy Austin. *The Assertive Woman.* San Luis Obispo, CA: Impact, 1987.

Schaef, Anne Wilson, and Diane Fassel. *The Addictive Organization: Why We Overwork, Cover Up, Pick Up the Pieces, Please the Boss, and Perpetuate Sick Organizations.* San Francisco: Harper and Row, 1990.

Thomas, Linda, Carol Pierce, Rick Huntley, Sharon Bueno Washington, David Wagner, & Lennox Joseph, *Journeys of Race and Culture: Paths to Valuing Diversity* (Laconia, NH: New Dynamics Publications, 1999). Graphic only.

Van Nostrand, Catherine Herr. *Gender-Responsible Leadership.* Newbury Park, CA: Sage, 1993.

West, Cornel. *Race Matters.* Boston: Beacon Press, 1993.

Wishik, Heather, and Carol Pierce. *Sexual Orientation and Identity: Heterosexual, Lesbian, Gay, and Bisexual Journeys.* Laconia, NH: New Dynamics Publications, 1995.

Zilbergeld, Bernie. *The New Male Sexuality.* New York: Bantam, 1992.

Colleagueship

Albrecht, Lisa, and Rose M. Brewer. *Bridges of Power: Women's Multicultural Alliances.* Santa Cruz, CA: New Society Publishers, 1990.

Belenky, Mary Field, Blythe McVieker Clinchy, Nancy Rule Goldberger, and Jill Mattuch Tarule. *Women's Ways of Knowing: The Development of Self, Voice, and Mind.* New York: Basic Books, 1988.

Campbell, Susan M. *The Couple's Journey: Intimacy as a Path to Wholeness.* San Luis Obispo, CA: Impact Publishers, 1980.

Eisler, Riane, and David Loye. *The Partnership Way: New Tools for Living and Learning, Healing Our Families, Our Communities, and Our World.* San Francisco: Harper, 1990.

Gilligan, Carol. *In a Different Voice: Psychological Theory and Women's Development.* Cambridge: Harvard University Press, 1993.

Heyward, Carter. *Touching Our Strengths: The Erotic as Power and the Love of God.* San Francisco: Harper and Row, 1989.

Hooks, Bell. Yearning: *Race, Gender, and Cultural Politics.* Boston: South End Press, 1990.

MacKinnon, Catharine A. *Toward a Feminist Theory of State.* Cambridge: Harvard University Press, 1991.

Ochs, Carol. *Women and Spirituality.* Totowa, NJ: Rowman and Allanheld, 1983.

Peck, Scott. *The Different Drum: Community Making and Peace.* New York: Simon and Schuster, 1988.

Pierce, Carol. *The Power Equity Group: A Guide for Understanding Equity and Acknowledging Diversity.* Laconia, NH: New Dynamics Publications, 1998

Steinem, Gloria. *Revolution from Within.* Boston: Little, Brown, 1992.

Wheatley, Margaret. *Leadership and the New Science.* San Francisco: Berrett-Koehler, 1992.

New Dynamics is a group of organization development consultants dedicated to helping to create organizations free of bias related to culture, gender, and sexual identitiy.

We believe we must live and practice what we expect others to value and live.

We believe that people can create for themselves a work environment which will nourish and productively utilize their special skills, and that organizations can create for all their employees a work environment that is challenging, growth-producing, and productive.

New Dynamics has met human resources training and consulting needs of clients since 1972. We serve business, industry, human services, and educational and religious institutions.

New Dynamics Publications is a voice for women and men of diverse races, cultures, and callings who experience life as a creative journey. We publish those expressions of the creative search for meaning that expand our boundaries. Our publications empower people to engage in a co-creative process.

PUBLICATIONS

A Male/Female Continuum: Paths to Colleagueship
Carol Pierce, David Wagner, and Bill Page, second edition 1994, 2004.

Sexual Orientation and Identity:
Heterosexual, Lesbian, Gay, and Bisexual Journeys
Heather Wishik and Carol Pierce, 1995.

Journeys of Race and Culture:
Paths to Valuing Diversity
Linda Thomas, Ph.D., Carol Pierce, Rick Huntley,
Sharon Bueno Washington, David Wagner, & Lennox Joseph, 1999.
(*book forthcoming, graphic available*)

Power Equity and Groups:
A Manual for Understanding Equity and Acknowledging Diversity
Carol Pierce, 1985, 1995, 2003.

For information write to: **New Dynamics Publications**
P.O. Box 595
Laconia, New Hampshire, 03247-0595
Fax 603 528-7912

Authors:

Carol Pierce, David Wagner, and **Bill Page** are innovators in addressing male/female issues in organizations. The foundation of their approach is the claiming of creative power through the developmental journeys of women and men.

Carol is known for her writings in the field of diversity work and for her development of the theory and practice of flat-structured or power equity groups. She is an organization development consultant specializing in process consultation since 1972. She lives in New Hampshire.

David's work as an organizational development and management consultant since 1976 continues to focus on diversity and power equity. He has served as Executive Director and Director of Operations in the health field and was a Coast Guard Officer. He lives in Vermont.

Bill has a unique base of experience which includes senior level management, extensive consulting in large organizations, and his work as an artist. Whether he is consulting on organizational performance, valuing diversity, or the creative process, Bill persists in opening new ground. He lives in New Mexico.

NOTES

NOTES

A Male/Female Continuum

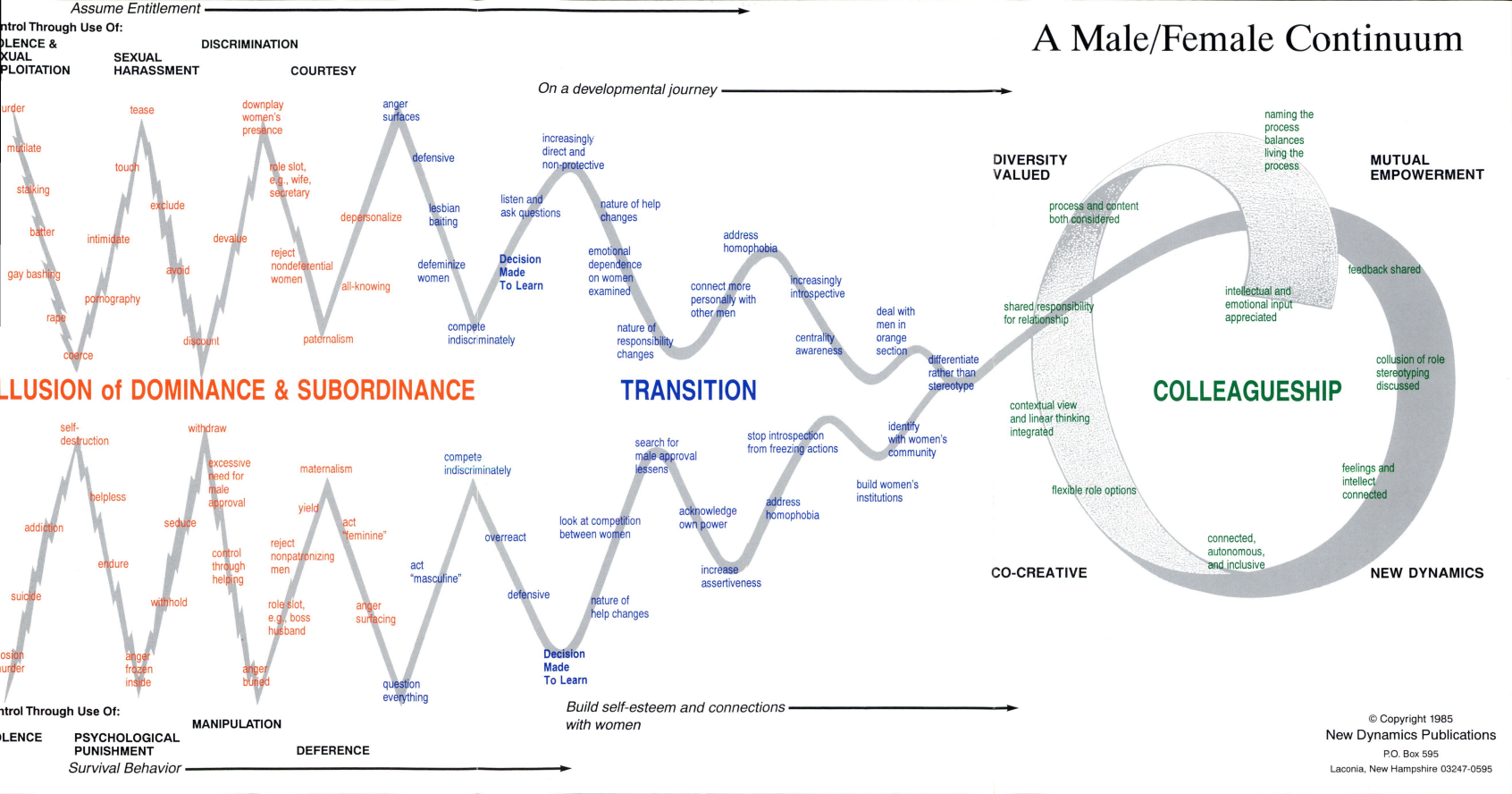

Assume Entitlement ⟶

ntrol Through Use Of:
OLENCE & XUAL PLOITATION

DISCRIMINATION

SEXUAL HARASSMENT

COURTESY

On a developmental journey ⟶

DIVERSITY VALUED

MUTUAL EMPOWERMENT

urder
mutilate
stalking
batter
gay bashing
rape
coerce

tease
touch
exclude
intimidate
avoid
discount

downplay women's presence
role slot, e.g., wife, secretary
depersonalize
reject nondeferential women
all-knowing
paternalism

anger surfaces
defensive
lesbian baiting
defeminize women
compete indiscriminately

increasingly direct and non-protective
listen and ask questions
nature of help changes
Decision Made To Learn
emotional dependence on women examined
nature of responsibility changes

address homophobia
connect more personally with other men
increasingly introspective
centrality awareness

deal with men in orange section
differentiate rather than stereotype

naming the process
balances living the process
process and content both considered
intellectual and emotional input appreciated
shared responsibility for relationship

feedback shared
collusion of role stereotyping discussed

LLUSION of DOMINANCE & SUBORDINANCE

TRANSITION

COLLEAGUESHIP

contextual view and linear thinking integrated
flexible role options

identify with women's community
build women's institutions

self-destruction
helpless
addiction
endure
suicide
osion urder

withdraw
excessive need for male approval
seduce
control through helping
withhold
anger frozen inside

maternalism
yield
act "feminine"
reject nonpatronizing men
role slot, e.g., boss husband
anger surfacing
anger buried

compete indiscriminately
overreact
act "masculine"
defensive
question everything

search for male approval lessens
look at competition between women
acknowledge own power
increase assertiveness
nature of help changes
Decision Made To Learn

stop introspection from freezing actions
address homophobia

CO-CREATIVE

connected, autonomous, and inclusive

feelings and intellect connected

NEW DYNAMICS

ntrol Through Use Of:
LENCE

PSYCHOLOGICAL PUNISHMENT

MANIPULATION

DEFERENCE

Build self-esteem and connections with women ⟶

Survival Behavior ⟶

© Copyright 1985
New Dynamics Publications
P.O. Box 595
Laconia, New Hampshire 03247-0595